Bright Liberty's Forgotten Sword
and the
Battle of Princeton

CPSIA information can be obtained
at www.ICGtesting.com
Printed in the USA
LVHW04s0236250518
578392LV00018BA/281/P

Bright Liberty's Forgotten Sword and the Battle of Princeton

John Lawrence Brasher

For my grandfather
Lawrence Dalrymple Watters (1878-1970)

And my mother,
Lois Ann Watters Brasher (1914-2013)

Table of Contents

Introduction

In 1825, the Marquis de Lafayette toured the United States celebrating the fiftieth anniversary of the start of the American Revolution. At a reception in Germantown, he was given a walnut snuff box inlaid with veneers from trees that had witnessed important historic American events. The donor, Philadelphia historian John Fanning Watson, included in the box a letter to Lafayette: "The love of relicks, connected with incidents on which the soul delights to dwell is a passion natural to man . . . and the reason is obvious. By such associations . . . minds are capable to commune with men and things of other times."[1]

When I visited my grandparents in Morristown, New Jersey, as a child, we often spent evenings looking at old family photographs. My grandparents gave story-voice to the portraits as well as to chairs, lamps, clocks, and tools that surrounded life in their home. The walnut side chair near the television was Grandma

---

1. John Fanning Watson to Deborah Norris Logan, July 20, 1825, Stenton Archives, in Laura C. Keim, "Remembering the 'Olden Time': John Fanning Watson's Cultivation of Memory and Relics in Early National Philadelphia," in George W. Boudreau and Margaretta Markle Lovell, *A Material World: Culture, Society, and the Life of Things in Early Anglo-America* (University Park, PA: The Pennsylvania State University Press, 2019), 294.

Caroline Pruden Clark's chair from Pruddentown, along Mount Kemble Avenue where bricks were made. Her son Lewis Clark was a mason and built fancy walls for the rich, including Thomas Nast, on Macculloch Avenue. He later became mayor of Morris Township. Caroline's unmarried daughter, "Aunt Mary" Clark, in old age moved in with her brother Lewis and his wife, Hattie. Hattie complained about Mary: "All she does is sit on her fat butt." Mary had a morbid fear of accidental death. Two brothers were alcoholic. One was killed while driving drunk. The other died from a tipsy fall out of a tree while picking cherries. Her brother Lewis, who never drank, opened the wrong door and instead of stepping onto a back porch lurched into the abyss of cellar stairs, fatally fracturing his skull. Mary, true to her fears, died one night when she fell out of bed. Her overweight impact on the floor killed her. The ogee clock in the front hall came from the fireplace mantel in the kitchen of the old farmhouse in Succasunna, New Jersey, where my grandfather Lawrence Watters grew up—the kitchen where the baking bread smelled so good and the bottom of the open-top Dutch door kept the chickens out. Lawrence's grandmother Ann Watters wrote her son Henry's name on the inside clock label. But Henry, who when he visited in Morristown embarrassed my mother as a "country bumpkin," died before his sister Loretta. When Ret came to live with my grandparents, the clock came with her.

The sword in my grandfather's study, however, spoke no stories from its early life. Generations of family leave-taking and resettlement silenced it. Forty years searching for clues to the original owner and maker of this heirloom Revolutionary War sword leaves me indebted to a host of helpers. I thank my grandparents and parents who imparted their interest in family and regional history. Their cherished mementos gave life to the past. And I am grateful for the providential day and place of my birth—July 4th in historic Morristown, New Jersey.

Some of this story previously appeared in the book *The Dog Head Sword of Succasunna: Forgotten Family Patriots and Loyalists in the Revolutionary War*. Recent discovery of documents detailing the location and life of Revolutionary War soldier Silus Watters calls for a different story. The sword probably did not belong to an obscure sometime-loyalist private, as the first book argued, but more likely was carried by a patriot militia captain, a hero of the Battle of Princeton. The narrative thread of the book is the search for the owner and maker of the sword. The story treats family, social, cultural, and political history as well as the sword itself. I am especially grateful to my graduate school mentor and friend Daniel W. Patterson, Kenan Professor of English and Chair of the Curriculum in Folklore at the University of North Carolina at Chapel Hill, who exemplified in his teaching and writing what John Fanning Watson knew before us—that material culture can open lost worlds, revealing past lives and societies to our minds and souls. For readers interested in a particular topic, any chapter can be read independently of the others.

Careful genealogical work is the supporting structure of this narrative. For that help, I thank Fred Sisser III, David Blackwell, William Stryker, Eleanor Romaine, Fred Emery, and William Tisch. The following curators generously shared their expertise and enthusiasm: Harold L. Peterson, Chief Curator of the National Park Service; Dr. Charles F. Montgomery, Curator of the Garvan and Related Collections of American Art, Yale University Art Gallery; Beatrice Garvan, Curator of American Decorative Arts, Philadelphia Museum of Art; Ann Wagner, Curator of Decorative Arts, Winterthur Museum. It was Ann Wagner who encouraged me to compose the history of the sword.

Collectors of American silver-hilted swords examined the sword for clues to its maker: Harold L. Peterson, Dr. John K. Lattimer, George C. Neumann, William H. Guthman, Daniel D. Hartzler, W. Kels Swan, John Dubozy, and John Sexton. Historians helped provide context: Theodore V. Brush, Phyllis B. D'Autrechy, Larry Kidder, Robert Selig, The Rev. Canon James Elliott Lindsley, Ben and Nancy Dontzin, who first gave me a tour of the Watters farm in Lebanon Township, New Jersey, Thomas Winslow and Eric Olsen of the Morristown National Historic Park, and Jude Pfister.

Archives and historical societies in New Jersey opened their collections that revealed fugitive details. Special thanks go to Roxanne Carkhuff of the Hunterdon County Historical Society, Fran Becker of the Washington Association of New Jersey, Joan Lucas of the Lebanon Township Historical Society, Margaret Bandrowski of the Springfield Historical Society, Margaret Cushing of the Roxbury Township Historical Society, Jessie Havens of Montgomery Township, Donald Sherblom of the 1759 Vought House, Linda Gilmore and The Rev. David Davis of Nassau Presbyterian Church, Paul Davis of the Historical Society of Princeton, and Joseph Klett and Bette Epstein of the New Jersey State Archives. The Pennsylvania Historical Society and the Department of Rare Books and Special Collections at Firestone Library, Princeton, provided valuable sources of information.

Dave and Sue Tullo welcomed me into their home to see Watters artifacts. Steve Higginbotham provided skillful copies of photographs. The text was improved throughout by my colleagues in the Department of History at Birmingham-Southern

College, Dr. Samuel N. Stayer and Dr. G. Ward Hubbs, and by my wife, Louise Tharaud Brasher. My son, Daniel Brasher, provided technical help.

Because my research spanned four decades, many who assisted me will not see this partial history of the sword. I hope that they have come to know the story in full.

JOHN LAWRENCE BRASHER

Bright Liberty's Forgotten Sword
and the
Battle of Princeton

And over this, no longer bright,
Though glimmering with a latent light,
Was hung the sword his grandsire bore.

Henry Wadsworth Longfellow,
Prelude, Tales of a Wayside Inn, 1863

CHAPTER 1

Surrender at Nassau Hall

To fight against the King,
Bright Liberty will bring.

James Moore, Marching Chant of the
Princeton Militia, 1776

In the summer of 2018, just a few feet from the grave of Aaron Burr in Princeton Cemetery, the buried fragments of James Moore's gravestone were discovered. A contemporary of Burr, Moore was lieutenant and captain of the Revolutionary War Princeton Militia. He lived on Nassau Street facing the College of New Jersey (now Princeton University) and was once as locally famous as Burr was notorious. The town and college celebrated him throughout his long life.

The battles of Trenton, December 26, 1776, and Princeton, January 3, 1777, saved the American Revolution. In December 1776, when Washington's troops retreated west across New Jersey before General Howe's pursuing army, the revolution was dying. But a week after the surprise victory at Trenton, Washington doubled his success by ambushing the British rear guard at Princeton. With Washington shouting "It's a fine fox chase my boys!," his troops routed the British in the fields near the village. The stunning wins at Trenton and Princeton turned the tide of the Revolution and inspired the Americans to keep fighting. English historian Sir George Trevelyan in 1909 summarized the two battles: "It may be doubted whether so small a number of men ever employed so short a space of time with greater and more lasting effects upon the history of the world." American historian Nathaniel Philbrick would call the victories "the greatest comeback of all time."[1]

Artifacts from the Battle of Princeton still emerge after two centuries. Metal detectors and computer georeferencing find lost battleground structures, rusty uniform buttons, and soldiers' graves. But this book is about a Battle of Princeton relic saved by a family for two centuries—a rare, silver-hilted, dog-headed sword, mascot of independence. Its story was lost not in soil and decay but in untimely deaths, filial lawsuits, and removal from its original community of memories.

This is how the battle ended. When General John Sullivan's Continental troops scattered the last lines of British regiments on Richard Stockton's hillside field above Frog Hollow, some of the British fled up the slope into Nassau Hall, hoping that behind its massive stone walls they could hold off their pursuers. They knocked out windows with their guns and prepared to make a stand. As Americans surrounded the building, young Captain Alexander

---

1. George Trevelyan, *The American Revolution*, vol. III, (New York: Longmans, Green, and Co., 1909), 136; Nathaniel Philbrick, "Valiant Ambition," *Annual Meeting of the Washington Association of New Jersey* (Morristown, NJ: The Board of Trustees of the Washington Association, 2018), 21.

Hamilton pulled up his artillery near to where Blair Arch stands today and opened fire. One six-pound shot shattered a window in the Prayer Hall and reputedly demolished the portrait of King George the Second. Another dented and rebounded from the south wall nearly killing American Major James Wilkinson's horse.[2]

While Hamilton's cannons pounded the back of the building, on the front side Princeton militia lieutenant James Moore drew his sword, rallied some cohorts, and stormed the door. He broke it open, attacked the regulars inside and shouted for their surrender.[3] A white flag appeared from a window. The British

---

2. James Wilkinson, *Memoirs of My Own Times* (Philadelphia: Abraham Small, 1816), 145.

3. The historical truth of Moore's action at Nassau Hall is sometimes questioned because of an absence of known contemporary sources and hitherto a lack of study of Moore. Several facts lend credence to the story. The earliest account discovered of Moore's storming the door, often overlooked, is in Barber and Howe (see n.4), which was recorded in 1842, only ten years after Moore's death, from Moore's contemporary Princeton neighbors and eyewitnesses. Although referred to as "Captain Moore" in the text, he was not yet captain of the Princeton militia at the time of the incident. Although some of Moore's company were in Pennington when the battle was fought, Moore was known to be in the Princeton area as a scout around the time of the battle. He stormed the door not with his official militia company but, as Barber and Howe say, "with some men," probably acquaintances, who were at the scene. Multiple events were happening at and near Nassau Hall concurrently—cannon balls smashing widows and walls, British regulars inside breaking out windows, Americans surrounding the building, other British troops fleeing through the town. With these actions happening at once, eyewitnesses evaluated the significance of each differently. Joseph Olden Clarke, born ca. 1800, of the Clarke family on whose farms the main battle was fought, related his family's war stories to Barber and Howe. Moore himself may have told Joseph Clarke the story of the surrender, or it may have been one of the Clarke family's stories. If the early account by Moore's contemporaries were fabulous, it would have been discounted in ensuing years by other local witnesses. See chapter five for more details.

strode out, "a haughty, crabbed set of men," followed by some liberated American prisoners—Continentals and thirty local "country people that were accused either of being rebels or aiding and assisting them."[4] The Battle of Princeton was over.

The surrender at Nassau Hall captured more than British soldiers. It captured the imagination of the patriots. The ten days of victories at Trenton and Princeton changed the course of the Revolution, and James Moore's bold charge crowned the renewed

Figure 1. Woodcut of Nassau Hall by James Tod, 1786, its first locally printed depiction. COURTESY OF DEPARTMENT OF RARE BOOKS AND SPECIAL COLLECTIONS, FIRESTONE LIBRARY, PRINCETON UNIVERSITY.

---

4. Account of Sergeant R [Root, Nathaniel], "The Battle of Princeton," from *The Phenix*, March 24, 1832, Wellsborough, PA, in The *Pennsylvania Magazine of History and Biography*, XX (1896), 518; Varnum Lansing Collins, ed., Robert Lawrence, *A Brief Narrative of the Ravages of the British and Hessians at Princeton in 1776-1777* (Princeton: The University Library, 1906), 34; John W. Barber and Henry Howe, *Historical Collections of the State of New Jersey* (Newark: Benjamin Olds, 1844), 272-273; John Frelinghuysen Hageman, *History of Princeton and Its Institutions* (Philadelphia: J.B. Lippincott and Co., 1879), Vol. I, 138.

American hope for "bright liberty." Nassau Hall itself soon symbolized the promise of the new nation. In its first local depiction
in a 1786 woodcut by Princeton printer, James Tod, turbulent
thunderclouds of war on the left of the cupola retreat to the East,
while placid clouds of peace on the right prevail from the West.[5]
The tale of Moore's brave exploit at Nassau Hall that ended the

---

5. Tod, a recent arrival from Scotland, was the first printer in Princeton and
was married to Anne French (b. 1762), the Scottish niece of John Witherspoon,
President of the college and minister of the Princeton Presbyterian Church. Liz
Hardie, "James Tod, Princeton 1784/New York," https://www.ancestry.com
/boards/surnames.tod/76/mb.ashx. Given the ties of Princeton to Yale—
Princeton presidents Aaron Burr, Sr., and Jonathan Edwards were both graduates
of Yale—the symbolic clouds of war and peace in the woodcut may be a reference
to a popular poem/war song written by Edwards' grandson Timothy Dwight,
graduate of and President of Yale 1795-1817. "Columbia" was written in 1778,
when Dwight was a chaplain in the Continental Army, and it was printed in
newspapers by 1780. Sydney Ahlstrom, historian of American religion, called the
poem "America's first national anthem." The celestial images of war and peace,
the new nation and the role of the scholar in it, fit well with Tod's woodcut of
Nassau Hall and its sky:

> As down a lone valley with cedars o'erspread,
> From war's dread confusion I pensively strayed;
> The gloom from the face of fair heaven retired;
> The winds ceased to murmur, the thunders expired.
> Perfumes as of Eden flowed sweetly along,
> A voice as of angels enchantingly sung,
> "Columbia, Columbia to glory arise,
> The queen of the world and the child of the skies."
>
> Fair science her gates to thy sons shall unbar,
> And the East see thy morn hide the beams of thy star;
> New bards and new sages unrivalled shall soar
> To fame unextinguished, when time is no more. . . .
> Columbia, Columbia, to glory arise,
> The queen of the world, and the child of the skies.

battle delighted listeners at New Jersey firesides and taverns for decades after the war. But as the voice of memory died, the story, like Moore's gravestone, sank into obscurity.

Figure 2. The gravestone of James Moore, Princeton Cemetery, before and after excavation in 2018. COURTESY OF NASSAU PRESBYTERIAN CHURCH.

"Murillo's Lesson," https://arnoldzwicky.org/2012/07/10/murillos-or-morellis -lesson/; Sydney Ahlstrom, "America's First National Anthem," sermon preached at Marquand Chapel, Yale University, Spring 1970, author's collection.

CHAPTER 2

The Saved and the Lost

The living know that they must die,
But all the dead forgotten lie;
Their memory and their sense is gone,
Alike unknowing and unknown.

Isaac Watts, 1707, A hymn sung
by Peter and Ann Watters, 1855[1]

I don't know why I never asked.

Lawrence Watters, 1969

The sword lay gathering dust on my grandfather's desk near a window overlooking the road from Morristown, New Jersey,

---

1. This hymn, like many others by Isaac Watts (1674-1748), became popular in New Jersey during the Great Awakening of the 1740s, as converts expressed their religious fervor by singing new evangelical hymns as well as the Psalms. It was a standard in Presbyterian congregations and was sung by five generations of the Watters family from the 1740s to the 1860s. The hymn is on page 31 in the well-worn hymnal of Peter and Ann Watters, *The Christian Minstrel* by J. B. Aiken (Philadelphia: T. K. Collins, 1855), author's collection.

to nearby Jockey Hollow. The tarnished silver dog head with wide eyes and grinning teeth that capped the sword's grip stared out of the eighteenth century. Scotch-taped on the wall above the desk, a magazine cover of newly elected President Eisenhower signified all was well. Close by, in a framed photograph of 1888, my ten-year-old grandfather, Lawrence Dalrymple Watters (1878-1970), stood with his grandmother and aunts and uncle against a picket fence in front of his grandparents' farmhouse on the dusty road from Flanders to Succasunna, New Jersey, ten miles west of Morristown. The old house, built in traditional East Jersey Cottage style, stood behind a huge sugar maple and had "lie-on-your-stomach" windows under the eaves. The sword was then on the attic floor of that house near those windows.[2] Every Fourth of July, grandfather Peter Watters brought it down for display. As a young man, he may have carried it in Independence Day parades.

My grandfather Lawrence grew up in his grandparents' home. His mother, Julia Adaline Leonard Watters (1853-1878) of nearby Mount Freedom, taught French at Schooley's Mountain Seminary. Three weeks after my grandfather was born, she died of "childbed fever." Her husband, Ezra (1854-1939), left the baby

---

2. The place name "Succasunna" derives from the Lenape words for "black": "suka," and for stone": "assun," indicating the abundance of iron ore in the area. The house still stands with its giant sugar maple on the northern corner of Unneberg Avenue and Honeyman Drive. Local history and architecture indicate that it was built by the Alpaugh family in the first half of the eighteenth century. The neighborhood was known locally as "Alpaugh" into the twentieth century, and the "Alpaugh School" stood within sight of the house. William Alpaugh, Succasunna, conversation with J. Lawrence Brasher, August 1978. The East Jersey Cottage style, located primarily in the Province of East Jersey, consisted of a story-and-a-half height with a gable over a three-bay façade with a side hall. Often, as in the Watters house, there was a stepped down kitchen wing to the side.

FIGURE 3. The farmhouse at Succasunna, 1888. Standing left to right: Ann Hance Watters (1826-1916), daughter Elizabeth Watters Green, daughter-in-law Harriet Watters (wife of James) with infant Howard, daughter Loretta Watters (1859-1947), grandson Lawrence Dalrymple Watters (1878-1970), son Henry Watters in wagon.

Figure 4. Julia Adaline Leonard Watters (1853-1878), 1877, who taught French at Schooley's Mountain Seminary.

Figure 5. Ezra Watters (1854-1939), ca. 1885.

with his parents, Ann Hance Watters (1827-1916) and Peter Lance Watters (1822-1888), and his nineteen-year-old unmarried sister, Loretta (1859-1947). They found a wet nurse, and kindhearted "Aunt Ret" filled in as virtual stepmother for "Lawrie." Ezra soon remarried, had more children, and took scant interest in my grandfather. He rarely visited. My grandfather resented him all his life.

Except for the sound of a distant train whistle, daily life on the Succasunna farm in the photo of 1888 differed little from that of the eighteenth century. The Watters' traditional skills and intense labor provided their food, clothing, and shelter. They followed centuries-old patterns of farm life, an economy of self-provisioning.[3] In the summer, both men and women rose before dawn and worked in the fields for two hours before returning for a typical breakfast of eggs, bread, fried potatoes, and fruit pies. Meat at breakfast was not common until the twentieth century. They spun wool and flax and poured

---

3. Richard Lyman Bushman, *The American Farmer in the Eighteenth Century: A Social and Cultural History* (New Haven: Yale University Press, 2018),4.

tallow candles. They raised chickens, turkeys, sheep for wool, hogs, apples, peaches, and cherries for themselves and to barter and sell. Wheat, rye, buckwheat, corn, potatoes, all manner of vegetables and berries, hops, flax, milk cows, and four workhorses supplied the rest of their needs.[4] As a young man, my grandfather hand cut wheat swinging a scythe with a grain cradle, threshed it with a flail and winnowed it on the breezy floor

Figure 6. Loretta "Aunt Ret" Watters (1859-1947), ca. 1885.

Figure 7. Candid scene at the farmhouse in Succasunna ca. 1900. Henry Watters and possibly Lawrence Watters sitting on steps, Grandmother Ann Hance Watters walking. Note the hops vine used in making beer arching in front of the porch.

---

4. Lawrence D. Watters, sound-recording, June 1969, author's collection.

Figure 8. Peter Lance Watters (1822-1888) of Little Brook, Lebanon Township, 1865.

Figure 9. Ann Hance Watters (1826-1916) of Little Brook, Lebanon Township, 1865.

between opposite open doors of the English style barn. He took books to the fields to study for school. The hands of the adults in the picket fence picture revealed their dawn to dusk toil. In 1947, when the last of them, Aunt Ret, died at my grandparents' Morristown home, the suburban funeral director placed a bouquet of flowers in her hands to hide their oversize, farm-worked form.[5]

Although smiles were not customary in nineteenth-century photographs, the dour stoicism of the Watters' faces in the farmhouse photo also bespoke their Scottish Calvinism and recent family misfortunes. Only a few months before the photograph was taken, just before the great blizzard of 1888, Peter Watters had died unexpectedly at age sixty-six from bronchial pneumonia and left behind an unpaid mortgage on the farm.

Both Peter and Ann Watters were born in Lebanon Township, Hunterdon County, New Jersey, on challenging terrain atop Schooley's

5. Lois Watters Brasher, conversation with J. Lawrence Brasher, March 2011.

Mountain. Peter and Ann began married life there in 1852 on a modest hillside farm in Little Brook, above Califon. Peter bartered to farm extra "patches" owned by Sarah and Susannah McLean, two elderly maiden sisters of his uncle Amos McLean (1790-1839).[6] Peter's parents, John (1787-1877) and Mary Elizabeth Lance Watters (1791-1882), lived a mile away in a large early nineteenth-century vernacular Georgian stone house, shaded by fashionable horse chestnut trees and set behind a fancy cast iron fence. Contemporary maps identified it as John Watters' "mansion house."[7] Married in 1810, John and "Lizzie" raised thirteen children, the last born when Lizzie was fifty-one.[8] John inherited some of his land and a distillery from his parents, Silus (1751-1820) and Sarah Savidge (1749-1833) Watters. As a young man, Silus served in the Revolution and kept a tavern near Princeton, New Jersey. He moved from Princeton to Lebanon Township by 1792 and amassed one of its largest farms of 640 acres. His older stone house still stands not far from his son John's also extant later house, near

Figure 10. John Watters (1787-1877) of Lebanon Township, 1865. Born in the tavern of Silus and Sarah Savidge Watters near Princeton.

6. Peter Watters Account Book, 1855-1868, author's collection; Theodore Frelinghuysen Chambers, *The Early Germans of New Jersey* (Baltimore: Genealogical Publishing Company, 1969), 556.

7. Ben Dontzin, conversation with J. Lawrence Brasher, March 1976.

8. Fred Emery, letter to J. Lawrence Brasher containing Watters family Bible record, February 21, 1972.

Figure 11. Mary Elizabeth Lance Watters (1791-1882) of Lebanon Township, 1865.

the summit of Mount Lebanon, the highest point in the township.[9]

The Watters served important roles in their community. In 1808, Silus Watters, "Esquire," was appointed Justice of the Peace by his cousin Governor Joseph Bloomfield.[10] After Silus's death in 1820, his son John held the same office and continually settled disputes in small claims court until at least the 1860s.

The lucrative family distillery was located at a spring between the houses of Silus and John. His previous work as tavern keeper in Princeton gave Silus expertise in quality spirits. From wagonloads of neighbors' apples and peaches and from local grain, the distillery produced cider, applejack, peach brandy, and whiskey.[11]

---

9. Silus Watters, Tavern Applications, 1788, 1790, Somerset County Tavern Applications, New Jersey State Archives; "Division of the late farm of Silas Watters, March 8, 1822," author's collection; Hunterdon County (NJ) Inventories, no. 3103J; West Jersey Deed Book A-Q, 474-476.

10. Justice of the Peace Certificate, Watters Papers, Lebanon Township Historical Society. Joseph Bloomfield and Silus Watters were both descended from Enoch Armitage (1677-1739), the first elder of the Pennington Presbyterian Church. Cyrus Armitage, *Some Account of the Family of Armitage* (London: Reed and Pardon Printers, 1850), 61-65. Silus Watters was a Justice of the Peace prior to this 1808 appointment. Documents in the Watters Papers list him as Justice in 1806. His older brother, Foster, was Justice of the Peace in Hopewell, NJ, 1816-1820. Justice of the Peace Docket of Foster Watters, Hunterdon County, NJ, New Jersey State Archives.

11. Silus Watters' "Appel Book" 1806, John Watters' "Apple Books" 1822, 1823, 1833, Watters Papers. The distillery was in production from the 1790s at

The substantial cash income from the distillery raised the Watters an economic step above their neighbors.

Lebanon Township was typical of nineteenth-century rural New Jersey. It was a traditional kinship community. Blended Scotch Irish and Palatine German families made their living on small farms. Watters, Hances, McLeans, and Beattys married Lantzes, Hoffmans, Hahns, and Swackhamers. Each new generation further strained the carrying capacity of the land, and inheritances

Figure 12. Joseph Bloomfield (1753-1823) by Charles Willson Peale. Governor of New Jersey, cousin of Silus Watters.

divided property into smaller and smaller lots. The legal fate of Silus's farm was typical. At his death in 1820, it was divided among his heirs into six parcels. At the close of the Revolutionary War, the same pattern of land division had pushed the Watters and their neighbors to Lebanon Township from more productive but crowded New Jersey farmland around Princeton and similar areas to the south and east. Lebanon's vacant, cheaper land, often already cleared of its forest to stoke the charcoal fires of the nearby Spruce Run and Musconetcong iron forges, attracted them.[12] But

---

least through the 1860s. In 1832, Lebanon Township had 11 distilleries, the most of any Hunterdon County township. In the 1790s, a 100 gallon still was worth a 200-acre farm. Harry B. Weiss, *The History of Applejack or Apple Brandy in New Jersey from Colonial Times to the Present* (Trenton: Agricultural Society, 1954), 146, 61.

12. For the iron forge industry, see Peter O. Wacker, *The Musconetcong Valley of New Jersey* (New Brunswick: Rutgers University Press, 1968); Sal Vuocolo, Jr., *The Ride to Pleasant Grove* (Flemington, NJ: D. H. Moreau Books, 1999).

many of the fields were steep and the soil thin. "Two stones grow to one dirt," the locals said.[13] The Watters improved their economy by operating the distillery and, after the Civil War, tending extensive peach orchards for the market.[14] But by the mid-1800s, a continuous outmigration of sons and daughters searching for room and riches left holes in the family fabric of Lebanon.

In 1869, Peter and Ann Watters followed his Aunt Rachel and Uncle John Trimmer's recent move off the mountain to Roxbury Township in Morris County, about fourteen miles as the crow flies northeast of Little Brook. They purchased a farm of eighty-five acres near Succasunna.[15] The soil there was the same as on the mountain, but deeper, and the land more gentle. Peter borrowed money from his father to buy the new farm, but their cash income, even from the better farm, was small. By the 1870s, self-provisioning, barter-and-exchange farming in the Northeast was on the wane, yet until the 1920s, Peter and Ann and their children persisted in living the old ways.

When Peter's father, John, died intestate in 1877, Peter's older brother, Ephraim Titus Watters, sued him for the $8,000 farm purchase loan that he owed their father's estate.[16] Not as resourceful, and jealous of Peter, Ephraim spent much of his youth wandering

---

13. A traditional saying recalled by Lebanon residents. Vuocolo, *The Ride to Pleasant Grove*, 86; Jeanne Robert Foster, *Adirondack Portraits, A Piece of Time* (Syracuse: Syracuse University Press, 1986), 37.

14. Ben Dontzin, conversation with J. Lawrence Brasher, March 1977.

15. Chambers, *Early Germans*, 555; Deed, John C. Willet to Peter L. Watters, April 7, 1869, author's collection.

16. Deed, William H. McDavit, Sheriff of Morris Country, NJ, Writ of *Fieri Facias* (Ephraim Watters vs. Peter L. Watters) to William H. Green, February 6, 1882, author's collection.

the "western country." He had no farm of his own. Peter thought the unpaid loan was his own rightful share of the estate. He could not pay, so Ephraim ordered a sheriff's sale of the Succasunna farm. Peter and Ann's son-in-law William Green, who had money, rescued them and bought the farm back for them, but they still owed a large debt to the estate. They mortgaged the farm to Daniel Lawrence Dalrymple (1826-1903), a wealthy farmer and iron master of Mount Freedom, favorite maternal uncle of my grandfather's late mother, and my grandfather's namesake. But major debt in a small-cash, self-provisioning economy was a disaster. Thirty years a widow, Ann Watters could never afford to pay more than interest on the loan. My grandfather remembered, "We took an interest payment to him every year, until there was no more money we could pay." According to Dalrymple's wishes, after his death, his common law wife of his later years forgave the debt.[17]

Figure 13. Ann Hance Watters (1826-1916), age 90, at the farm in Succasunna, 1916, with her great-granddaughter Lois Ann Watters (1914-2013).

My mother, born 1914, fondly remembered her visits to the farm when she was a child. My grandparents took her on the trolley from Morristown ten miles to Succasunna, where my grandfather's

---

17. Lawrence D. Watters, sound recording, June 1969; Ann Watters and Peter L. Watters to Daniel Lawrence Dalrymple, Bond, March 7, 1882, author's collection.

Uncle Henry was waiting for them with a horse and wagon. They would arrive on the fine dust road in front of the farmhouse kitchen just as Aunt Ret was taking bread out of the wood stove oven, and Ret would cover it with churned butter that melted on the warm bread. They ate the bread and drank milk that had cooled in stone crocks kept in the basement. At night, my mother slept in a cozy feather tick under the eaves and looked out the low windows at the stars twinkling through the limbs of the ancient sugar maple that still stands today in front of the house.

On April 18, 1918, a year after Ann Watters' death at 90, her son Henry held a public auction at the farm of some of her effects.[18]

Figure 14. Lawrence Dalrymple Watters (1878-1970) with his dog "Friday" at the farm in Succasunna, ca. 1915.

---

18. Jacob W. Baker, Auctioneer, receipt for sale, to Henry Watters, April 18, 1918, author's collection.

My grandfather bought her flax wheel. Later, while the crowd continued to bid on items, he quietly slipped up to the attic and took the dog head sword.

Lawrence Watters' favorite poet was Henry Wadsworth Longfellow. He knew the poetic significance of the April 18th date of the sale, immortalized in Longfellow's *Tales of a Wayside Inn*, "The Landlord's Tale: Paul Revere's Ride." The date likely heightened his resolve to take the Revolutionary relic. He enjoyed reciting the first verse:

Listen my children and you shall hear
Of the midnight ride of Paul Revere.
On the eighteenth of April in Seventy-five;
Hardly a man is now alive
Who remembers that famous day and year.

The *Interlude* before the other tales spoken by visitors at the inn concludes:

The landlord ended thus his tale.
Then rising took down from its nail
The sword that hung there, dim with dust,
And cleaving to its sheath with rust,
And said, 'This sword was in the fight.[19]

---

19. Lawrence Watters graduated from Trenton State Normal College for teachers in 1899. He served as principal of schools in Bartley, Green Village, and Morris Township, New Jersey, until 1910, when he married Bessie Swackhamer Clark (1885-1973), daughter of Lewis E. and Harriet Skellenger Swackhamer Clark. Lewis Clark was longtime mayor of Morris Township. Lawrence gave Bessie a book of the complete works of Longfellow as a wedding gift. After his marriage, Watters left teaching and worked for two years at the U.S. Customs Office in New York City. Then he returned to Morristown and worked for

My grandfather never knew that his own great-great-grandfather Silus Watters kept a tavern in Princeton where similar stories were told.

In the 1920s, brother and sister Uncle Henry and Aunt Ret Watters were too old to work the Succasunna farm, and they sold it to a city businessman for use as a summer home. Later bought by a developer in the 1950s, the fields were divided into small lots and roads and were covered with split-level houses by 1960. Suburban sprawl fragmented even the ancient hillside woodlot into lawns and pavement and named it Beechwood Drive. When my grandfather was 90 years old, I took him in the car to see the farmhouse where he grew up. We didn't get out to walk, but just before we pulled away he said, "Wait a minute." He opened the car door, turned in his seat, and put his feet on the ground once more.

When I was a child, he would show me the sword. Lifting it from the desk clutter, he would say, "This was used in the Revolutionary War." Then he would pull it out of its scabbard and point

---

three decades until retirement in the U.S. Post Office near the Green. He served as treasurer of Morris Township for 36 years. A patriotic student of Revolutionary War history, he assigned his classes stories of Tempe Wick, John Honeyman, and Molly Pitcher from the popular newly published *Stories of New Jersey* (New York: American Book Company, 1896) by Frank Stockton. The house he built in 1917 in Morris Township, on Center Avenue at the top of Lovell Avenue, stands just over the ridge east of Henry Knox's 1779-1780 artillery park. It has a commanding eastward view of Western Avenue and Fort Nonsense. Some of my fondest childhood memories are of visits with my grandparents to the nearby "Tempe Wick house," the ancient Bettin oak, and the Ford Mansion. In Jockey Hollow, my grandmother would point out the house of her ancestor Joshua Guerin whose farm bordered the Wick farm and provided pasture for horses in Washington's army.

Figure 15. Brother and sister Uncle Henry and Aunt Ret Watters (1859-1947) at the farm in Succasunna with dog "Friday" ca. 1915. Note the early nineteenth-century English style hay barn and wood pile, left rear.

to dark spots on the blade: "They always said it had blood stains on it."

On July 4, 1960, my thirteenth birthday, my grandfather gave me a package tied with a red, white, and blue ribbon. It was the sword. I loved family history and was always pestering him with questions. He himself was what folklorists call a "tradition bearer." He described his own boyhood life on his grandparents' farm in rich detail. In old age he once grew a few stalks of wheat next to his backyard vegetable garden in Morristown, so he could show me what as a boy he sweated in the fields to harvest. But he knew little earlier lore about his family. He remembered conversations that before Succasunna his grandparents had lived at a place in Hunterdon County near Califon called Little Brook, on Schooley's Mountain. The sword came down through the family, but he had no idea who carried it in the Revolution. "I don't know why I never asked," he lamented. Events beyond my grandfather's control lost the stories of his ancestors, yet saved some remarkable heirlooms.

Both his great-grandfather John Watters (1787-1877) and his great-great Revolutionary War grandfather, Silus Watters (1751-1820), died intestate. By the 1890s, the family had forgotten that the maiden name of Silus's wife, Sarah, was Savidge.[20] The incertitude about family history was due in part to grandfather Peter Watters' unexpected death, when Lawrence was only ten. Peter's early death drew a curtain between the Lebanon and Succasunna chapters, shrouding the prior life of the family. And the earlier estate lawsuit over Peter's farm loan was bitter. Although they were devout Presbyterians—if it rained all week and cleared on Sunday, they would not work on the Sabbath—the Watters nevertheless had hot tempers and carried grudges. Ann Watters said she hated to see her own daughter Liz coming up the road, because her visits were so contentious.[21] The lawsuit between Peter and his older brother, Ephraim, silenced talk about prior family life in Lebanon, and the estrangement between my grandfather and his own father, Ezra, shut the door on Ezra's memories. Yet had my grandfather not been taken by his father to live on the farm with his grandparents, he probably

---

20. In Chambers *Early Germans*, published in 1895 and much of it based on interviews with descendants, the family incorrectly wondered if her surname were "Lyons," 555.

21. Lawrence Watters, sound-recording, June 1969.

would not have known about the sword and saved it from the auctioneer's gavel.

When I was a teenager, the sword hung proudly over my bedroom desk. An antiques dealer said it was an interesting piece of early American silver. When the Bicentennial came, I decided to find out more. The first book I looked at said dog-headed swords are the most rare of eighteenth-century American silver-hilted swords.

CHAPTER 3

The Sword

The 'most unique' of the iconic American silver dog-head officer's swords.

John Sexton, American Arms Historian, 2017

You may not know who your sword belonged to," the curator said, "but he was darn rich."[1] In 1775, a silver-hilted sword cost five pounds or more. That was five month's salary for a rank-and-file British soldier, over twice the annual pay of a ship hand, or now, several thousand dollars.[2] It is a hunting sword, a civilian arm called a "cuttoe" by the English, from the French "couteau

---

1. W. Kels Swan, President, the Swan Historical Foundation, conversation with J. Lawrence Brasher, June 12, 2010.

2. John J. McCusker, *How Much Is That in Real Money?* (Worcester, MA: American Antiquarian Society, 2001). An ad in the *New Jersey Gazette*, Trenton, July 1, 1778, states: "Mrs. Livingston [wife of Governor Livingston] of Princeton advertises a sword lost between Princeton and Morristown; offers ten dollars reward." In the estate inventory of Phillip Dumont of Hopewell tallied by Foster Watters (brother of Silus) in May 1814, the second listing is a "Silver Headed Sword" valued at fourteen dollars. Hunterdon County Will no. 2656.

de chasse." Not originally designed as military weapons, they first were worn in the colonies as part of civilian dress by "those who could afford the luxury of silver."[3] In a stratified society, the gentry displayed their standing by wearing such swords, some owning special black or purple sword belts to be worn during mourning. Gentlemen were even described as "naked" if they appeared in public without their swords.[4]

A few hundred American silver-hilted swords, from the crude to the finely wrought, exist in museums and private collections. The largest number were in the collection of the late Dr. John K. Lattimer.[5] The first silver hilts date from the early 1700s, and by the end of the century, they already were passing out of fashion. Those with animal-figure pommels are considered the finest. Three types are known, the lion head found well before and during the Revolutionary War, the eagle pommel of the later Federal period, and the dog head produced on the eve of and through the war, a symbol of patriot sentiments rejecting the British lion. The dog head has always been the rarest of the three. At the first major exhibition of American silver hilts, held in 1954 at the Corcoran Gallery of Art, Washington, D.C., only two were known. Since then, the number of known finely crafted dog heads has climbed to perhaps ten.[6]

---

3. Harold L. Peterson, *The American Sword 1775-1946* (Philadelphia: Ray Riling Arms Book Co., 1980), 211.

4. David Hackett Fischer, *Albion's Seed: Four British Folkways in America* (New York: Oxford University Press, 1989), 359.

5. See Daniel D. Hartzler, *Silver Mounted Swords, The Lattimer Collection* (State College, PA: Josten's Printing Company, 2000).

6. The exhibition was organized by Harold Peterson, then dean of American sword scholars. When he examined the Watters sword in 1976, he wrote:

This sword, like most American silver hilts, has no maker's mark. Especially during the Revolution, some armorers for the patriot cause did not want to reveal themselves to the British. Though artfully fashioned, some of the silver features of the sword are not quite as finely engraved as those made by noted makers Ephraim Brasher and John Bailey, indicating craftsmanship of a young or journeyman silversmith. Topped with a doorknob-style capstan, the hilt has a turned, spiral-channeled, ivory grip stained dark green with arsenic, the ivory an added sign of wealth. The pommel is a finely executed hound's head with some features that differ from other dog heads: a broad nose and muzzle; bared, rectangular, human-like teeth either snarling or grinning; prominent eyelids and human-like eyes looking straight up at the wearer or

Figure 16. The dog head with rectangular teeth, folded ears, pairs of chasing marks on the cheeks, deeply engraved hair on the neck.

"Congratulations on owning a very, very fine sword." Peterson, *American Sword*, 30; Harold L. Peterson, letter to J. Lawrence Brasher, September 14, 1976.

anyone who approached when the sword was in position in its scabbard belt; large ears folded into an oval; pairs of tiny chasing marks possibly to denote hair on the nose, cheeks, and jowls; much denser, deeply engraved hair on the neck and between the ears, like a furry mane (figure16). A simple ferrule sets off the neck from the ivory grip. A stud ring protrudes from under the chin for a missing chain guard that passed from the head to a ring at the rear of the oval floating guard. On all other similar swords, upper chain guard stud rings are either on the collar ferrule or held in the dog's teeth. Chain guards were often broken during combat, but sometimes they were deliberately removed to accommodate a large hand.[7] The lower grip ferrule features two unusual bands, the upper, wider one engraved with repeated triangular

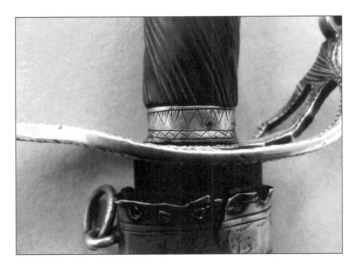

Figure 17. The lower ferrule of the grip with rectangular points and cross hatching.

7. H. Kels Swan, personal conversation with J. Lawrence Brasher, June 12, 2010.

points or leaf tips, the lower one with somewhat irregular cross hatching (figure 17).

The oval, four-slotted floating hand guard is thicker than most other similar ones. The obverse (outside) edge is sharply scalloped, while the reverse (inner) edge, worn next to the leg, is smooth. A display of bright cut engraving completely covers both the upper and lower surfaces of the guard.

A distinctive, angular, feather-edge pattern that gives a clue to the sword's maker appears on the upper and lower surfaces of the reverse edge: a center line runs the length of the edge, the inner side engraved with parallel cuts at right angles to the center line, the outer side also cut with opposing parallel lines but at a slanting angle to the center line. The overall effect is that of a skewed but attractive herringbone pattern (figures 18, 19, 20). At

Figure 18. The upper, inner side of the guard with skewed herringbone pattern, saltire, band of double chasing marks, and sunburst flaring from the base of the grip.

Figure 19. The underside of the guard with stylized foliage (left), skewed herringbone pattern, band of double chasing marks, and sunburst from the center. Probable combat damage to the guard, upper right.

the front of the guard, top and bottom, the center lines of the pattern flow into forms of elongate, stylized foliage (Figure 19).

The margins of the four openings in the guard are delicately chased with bands of tiny double indentations like strung beads (figures 18, 19, 20). On both the upper and lower surfaces, a sunburst of rays flares out from the center of the guard to its sides and tips (figures 18, 19, 20). Finally, the guard features in high relief four saltires, an x-shape known among the Scotch Irish as Saint Andrew's cross. One of them, on the lower side of the rear tip, is highlighted in the center of a swirl of spinning rays (figure 20). The outside edge of the guard is broken, smashed in toward the grip possibly from a blow struck in combat—or perhaps from the impact of breaking open a door.

The hilt is 5 ¾ inches long, the American steel blade 26 inches, with a simple fuller and a false edge. The original leather scabbard survives with silver top and middle mounts, each with parallel line decorations and a carrying ring. The tip, which was

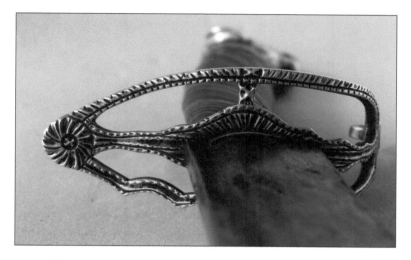

Figure 20. The underside of the guard with saltire in a swirl, skewed herringbone pattern, two other saltires, band of double chasing marks, and sunburst from the center.

probably also silver, is missing. Single tooled lines on the leather follow the edges on the outside of the scabbard, which is stitched on the inside to each side of a full-length center strip of leather.

The silver top mount of the scabbard is engraved on the inner side with the script initials of the owner, JM, in a finely ornamented style popular at the time of the Revolution.[8] Centered above the initials and the parallel decorative lines is the date 1775, the year when many in New Jersey were arming themselves for

---

8. The initials are a close match to those in the pattern book of John Russell, *A complete and useful book of cyphers: where the various combinations of the alphabet are ornamentally disposed in the present taste; beautifully engraved on twenty-four copper plates.* (London: Robert Sayer, 1775). Although I and J were interchangeable in some eighteenth-century type and writing, in the script of this and other period pattern books, they are distinct.

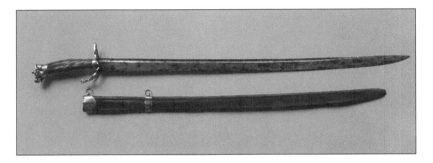

Figure 21. The sword and scabbard.

the coming conflict.[9] On the sides of the date are five crude holes punched through the silver at a later time, not by the maker, to sew it to the scabbard. Remains of the thread are in the leather. These holes to secure the scabbard indicate considerable wear and tear on the sword, constant use in the field by its owner, not just use as symbolic dress for genteel occasions. To the right of the date, both the upper half of the silver top mount and the scabbard behind it are split apart vertically, again, possibly combat damage.

Silver-hilted hunting swords provided officers in the Revolution a way to display their rank at dress and ceremonial occasions.[10] But Washington also required officers to wear swords in action "as a mark of distinction and to enable them the better to maintain the authority due to their stations."[11]

Although the sword is an officer's sword, at the beginning of the war and in pre-war militia drills, some well-to-do men who were not officers carried their dress swords. Men with money in

---

9. In the eighteenth century, the numeral 1 was sometimes carved, printed, or written as a J. The J shape on the sword may be intended, or it may be a gouge.

10. George Neumann, letter to J. Lawrence Brasher, December 12, 1979.

11. John C. Fitzpatrick, ed., *The Writings of George Washington* (Washington, D.C., 1931-44), vol.18:45, "Letter to the Board of War," 23 February 1780.

Figure 22. The top mount of the scabbard with initials
JM, date 1775 above, and holes punched by the owner to
sew the mount to the scabbard. The vertical split in the
silver and leather behind is possible combat damage.

citizen militia companies eagerly purchased fancy swords, often
cuttoes, to prepare for hostilities. Although traditionally not meant
for battle, cuttoes were still a common and formidable weapon at
close conflict.[12] New York silversmith Charles Oliver Bruff, later
a loyalist, specializing in sword-hilting, aimed his July 8, 1776,
newspaper ad at all who could afford his work: "Those Gentlemen
who are forming themselves into Companies in Defense of their
Liberties, and others that are not provided with SWORDS, May
be suited therewith by applying to Charles Oliver Bruff. . . . Small
Swords Silver mounted; Cut and Thrust and Cutteau De Chase,

12. George Neumann, *Swords and Blades of the American Revolution* (Har-
risburg, PA: Stackpole Books, 1973) 51.

mounted with beautiful green Grips, and Broad Swords as Gentlemen may fancy. . . . Lyon Heads, Dog Heads, Bird Heads, &c. being a collection of the most elegant Swords ever before made in America. . . . Scabbards made for Swords, at the shortest Notice, at different prices. All Gentlemen of the American Army who are not supplied may have them at the above Shop."[13]

In 1775, the Continental Congress recommended that the states require all men in their militias to carry bayonets as well as either swords or hatchets. In April of that year, the journal of a Minute Man who marched to Lexington included in his list of equipment "A Scabbard & Belt Therefor [sic] A Cuting [sic] Sword."[14]

13. *New York Gazette* and the *Weekly Mercury*, July 8, 1776, in John R. S. Dobozy, "Charles Oliver Bruff, Tory Silversmith and Sword Cutler of Maiden Lane," *Man at Arms* (22), June 2000: 35.

14. Journal of Arthur Harris, Bridgewater, Massachusetts, 1775, William H. Guthman Collection in Neumann, *Swords*, 24, 20.

CHAPTER 4

Searching for Provenance

You are standing on his front porch.
Ben Dontzin, Lebanon Township, December 1976.

The mute dog head pointed to several contestants in my search for the original owner of the sword. The hound led me to museums, archives, and historic houses, and introduced me to curators, collectors, historians, tour guides, military reenactors, and genealogists. On the way, we sometimes sniffed out trails that got us lost but nevertheless took us to interesting places. Some of the stories, though not the particular story of the sword, are worth telling.

The JM initials were a puzzle. No one in the family remembered any surnames of relatives beginning with "M." A sketchy note in my grandfather's hand, probably copied from the 1895 genealogy classic, *Early Germans of New Jersey*, showed that my great-great-great-great-grandfather Silus Watters (1751-1820) was of the Revolutionary generation. Did he carry the JM sword? If Silus carried it in the war, why didn't his name stick to it? If so, how did he acquire it and from whom? Did he pick the sword up on a battlefield? Did a friend give it to him? Arms historians claim that such prized swords were not usually pilfered from battlefields, and most were passed down in families through wills and estate sales or received as gifts from friends.

The first known owner was Peter Watters (1822-1888), Silus's grandson, who, when he moved from his family community on Schooley's Mountain in 1869, was really a latecomer to Succasunna. I assumed that Peter already had the sword from his grandfather when Peter lived in Little Brook. When Peter and Ann moved by wagons to Succasunna, they brought along all sorts of household furnishings from Lebanon—cupboards, chests, and decorative objects as well as utilitarian goods. Some were heirlooms from at least their grandparents' generation.[1]

I started the search for JM with *Early Germans of New Jersey* that traced the family to Silus Watters and his son John of Lebanon. The book stated that two of Silus Watters' daughters, first Polly, then Betsey, had married Amos McLean. Polly and Betsey were aunts, and Amos was twice uncle, of Peter Watters. I found in the will of Priscilla Titus Watters (Silus's mother) that Silus had a brother-in-law William Morgan. So two "M" surnames surfaced. First, I wanted to see the place where the Watters had lived in Lebanon Township.[2]

On a December afternoon in 1976, I left my home in Stillwater, Sussex County, New Jersey, to look for Little Brook, Peter and Ann Watters' former community. I drove the winding road west from Califon and Lower Valley up the slopes of Schooley's

---

1. Personal collection of author.

2. Chambers, *Early Germans*, 556; Hunterdon County Will no. 2233.

Mountain to where the map said Little Brook. Not much there. I continued on to Anthony Road, and the way began to have an ancient feel to it, a meandering lane often sunk below the bordering overgrown fields and lined with aged sugar maples, a track worn deep by centuries of horse and wagon traffic. I began to have a strange feeling that I was approaching some determined destination—almost a palpable sensation of being led. Early stone houses crowded the narrow road. I stopped at two, walking makeshift plank paths over mud and asked the people if they knew anyone named Watters. They didn't.

Then a sign at the bottom of a steep driveway on the right: "Stillwatter Farm." Two "t's"? I turned up the wooded lane, and after climbing a quarter mile, emerged on a level expanse with a sweeping view of a beautiful fieldstone house framed by venerable

Figure 23. The "mansion house" of John and Mary Elizabeth Lance Watters, Anthony Road, Lebanon Township, December 1976.

horse chestnut trees. When I knocked at the door, a jolly man greeted me with a quizzical smile. I told him I was looking for the home of my ancestor John Watters. "You are standing on his front porch!" he said.

Ben Dontzin welcomed me in to meet his wife, Nancy, a schoolteacher. Both loved history and had researched whatever they could of the house and surroundings. Nancy had rescued fallen fragments of Silus Watters' gravestone epitaph from the grass mowers of the nearby Pleasant Grove Presbyterian Church cemetery and kept them reassembled like a jigsaw puzzle on top of her grand piano! She and Ben showed me an early nineteenth-century slipware chamber pot they had unearthed from a former

Figure 24. An early nineteenth-century slip ware chamber pot excavated from a privy site at the home of John and Mary Elizabeth Lance Watters, Lebanon Township. COURTESY DAVID AND SUE TULLO.

Figure 25. The house of Silus and Sarah Savidge Watters on Mount Lebanon Road, Lebanon Township, December 1976.

Watters privy site and had glued back together. They walked me to the nearby foundations of Silus's distillery, and told me how to drive around to his eighteenth-century stone house that still stood just over the hill on Mount Lebanon Road.[3]

Nancy recalled that somewhere she had read that a "Colonel Morgan" sold Silus part of his farm. They also told a local tale that when Silus's house was remodeled some years back, the owner allegedly had uncovered a secret underground room that contained Revolutionary War uniforms that he gave to Washington's

---

3. "Stillwatter Farm" referenced both the family name and the distillery. Later, I discovered in Sal Vuocolo's *The Ride to Pleasant Grove*, that the farm and extant stone house of James Hance (1772-1857), grandfather and benefactor of Peter Watters' wife, Ann Hance, joins the Watters farm on the west.

Headquarters in Morristown. In forty years of research, I never found "Colonel Morgan," and a phone call to the remodeler, who had moved to California, revealed that he discovered only a boarded-up basement alcove with nothing in it. But all in all, it was an exciting start.[4]

Joseph Morgan (1728-after 1786)

Silus Watters' sister Martha married William Morgan. The Morgans were a large and distinguished family, a promising lineage for gentry and military officers. During the Revolution, they lived near the Watters in Hopewell, adjoining Princeton, and when Silus moved from Princeton to Lebanon, William and Martha moved there too, taking care of Martha's and Silus's aged mother, Priscilla, and purchasing part of Silus's new "plantation."

William Morgan was the grandson of the famous, or infamous, minister Joseph Morgan (1674-1741), pastor of the Pennington Presbyterian Church (1729-1737) in Hopewell, where the Watters then worshipped. A member of the first graduating class at Yale, Joseph Morgan published numerous books, some from Benjamin Franklin's press, and he corresponded in Latin with the eminent Massachusetts divine, Cotton Mather.[5] But his

---

4. John Denton, telephone conversation with J. Lawrence Brasher, March 2, 1985.

5. Ebenezer Baldwin, *Annals of Yale College, from its Foundation to the Year 1831* (New Haven: B. & W. Noyes, 1838), 3; James Steen, "The Rev. Joseph Morgan, Pastor of the Presbyterian Church of Freehold and Middletown. 1709-1731," in *The Presbyterian Church of Freehold and Middletowne, New Jersey* (Freehold, NJ: Freehold Transcript, 1907), 3.

brilliance suffered from personal excesses. In 1728, his Freehold, New Jersey, flock dismissed him for having "practiced astrology, countenanced promiscuous dancing, and transgressed in drink." The Pennington church in 1736 likewise suspended him from ministry for intemperance. His preaching was learned, but maybe too enthusiastic—"taking five drams before sermon."[6] He reportedly repented during the Great Awakening under the nearby Maidenhead and Amwell preaching of the dramatic English itinerant, George Whitefield. Joseph Morgan died in 1741 preaching along the New Jersey coast.[7]

Of Joseph's ten children, Andrew (1703-1791) of Hopewell, uncle of Silus's brother-in-law William Morgan, was very wealthy. He owned several farms in Hunterdon and Somerset counties and bought silver buckles from nearby Trenton silversmith John

---

6. Edwin G. York, *The Pennington Area Presbyterians 1709-1984* (Pennington, NJ: Pennington Presbyterian Church, 1985), 73.

7. George Whitefield (1714-1770) was the most famous itinerant preacher of the eighteenth century and the most well-known figure in the colonies at the beginning of the Revolution. His dramatic "field preaching" is legendary. Benjamin Franklin reported that Whitefield preached to 8,000 people in the open air in Philadelphia and estimated that he could be heard by 30,000. In 1739, Whitefield preached to 1500 from the back of a wagon at Maidenhead, Hunterdon County, New Jersey, and in 1740, to 3,000 outside the Presbyterian Church at Amwell, Hunterdon County. Some historians claim that his egalitarian theology paved the way for the Revolution. James Wilson and John Fiske, eds., *Appleton's Cyclopedia of American Biography* (New York: Appleton & Co., 1887-1889), 390; Luke Tyerman, *The Life of the Rev. George Whitefield* (New York: Anson D. F. Randolph, 1877), 331; Thomas S. Kidd, *George Whitefield: America's Spiritual Founding Father* (New Haven: Yale University Press, 2014), 93; *A Continuation of The Rev. Mr. Whitefield's Journals* (London: W. Strahan, 1741), 27.

Fitch.[8] Andrew was a friend and business associate of notable Trenton resident General Philemon Dickinson (1739-1809), who purchased a silver-hilted cuttoe from Fitch in 1775.[9]

In contrast to his brother Andrew, Moses Morgan (ca. 1705-1775) of Hopewell, father of Silus's brother-in-law William Morgan, left almost no historical record and possessed no notable assets. But along with William, Silus's brother-in-law, Moses did have a son named Joseph, a possible JM of the sword's vintage. Researching Joseph turned up disappointingly little. Born about 1728, he was listed as a trustee of the Pennington Presbyterian Church in 1762, indicating some status.[10] In 1772, he was appointed overseer of the highways in Hopewell and lived on a modest 41 acres. In 1785, he purchased and moved to 125 acres in Lebanon Township, preceding Silus Watters there, but after 1786, Joseph's trail disappeared.[11] No military records match this Joseph. Nothing survives that shows any ongoing relationship between Joseph Morgan and his brother William Morgan or Silus Watters. No attractive evidence connects the sword to this JM or his Morgan family.

8. John Fitch Account Book, 1773-1776, August 18, 1775, John Fitch Papers, no. 0208, Historical Society of Pennsylvania.

9. John Fitch Account Book, August 24, 1775; Hunterdon County Mortgage Book I, 178.

10. York, *Pennington Presbyterians*, 73.

11. Lida Cokefair Gedney, *The Town Records of Hopewell, New Jersey* (New Jersey Society of Colonial Dames, 1931), 32; Kenn Stryker-Rodda, "New Jersey Tax Rateables, 1778-1780," in *The Genealogical Magazine of New Jersey* (48), 43; "A List of the Assessment from the Township of Lebanon (Hunterdon County, NJ), June 1785, July and August 1786," New Jersey State Archives, Trenton.

John McLean (1751-1811) or James McLean (1755-after 1804)

The hound next led me to the McLeans on a long poorly marked path. Peter Watters' "twice" uncle, Amos McLean (1790-1839), who married Peter's aunts Polly and Betsy Watters, was the son of William McLean, Jr., (1760-1848) and Sarah Curle McLean of Kingwood, New Jersey. William McLean, Jr., did not serve in the Revolution, even though he was of legal age to enlist in 1776, but his two older brothers, James and John, did.[12] There were even two swords—valued along with a gun for a total of only four dollars—listed in the estate inventory of Amos McLean in 1839. But when Amos's uncles James and John McLean died in the early 1800s, their estates were modest. They were at most middling farmers, not then typical owners of silver-hilted swords.

I early left the trail of the McLeans as too poor to own a silver-hilted sword, but a chance reading of a will led back to the McLeans.[13] In his will of April 4, 1777, John King, a widower of Bedminster Township, Somerset County, ordered that some of his estate be left to his grandchildren including those "of my daughter Isabella, the wife of William McLean, Sr."[14] The brothers James and John McLean were John King's grandsons and his beneficiaries.[15]

---

12. "Curl Family of Warren Co., NJ, 1780-1850," http://www.genealogy.com/forum/surnames/topics/curl/947/; "Curl," http://genforum.genealogy.com/curl; Abstract of New Jersey Wills vol. V (1771-1780), Will, November 8, 1775.

13. Harold O. Pruden, "McLean," typescript, 1937, Morristown, New Jersey, Public Library.

14. Somerset County Will no. 510.

15. Chambers, *Early Germans*, 584.

King was one of the wealthiest men of Somerset County at the time of the Revolution.[16] The estate inventory of his personal effects, alone, including "a negro man named Joseph" and a "negro boy named Harry," came to the weighty sum of 1068 pounds, 6 shillings, and 7 pence. King was a presiding elder of the Lamington Presbyterian Church, and he paid one of the highest rents "for his seat," entitling him to an entire pew.[17]

From 1772 to 1775, King governed as a Chosen Freeholder for Somerset County, and at the start of the war, he was a member of the Committee of Inspection charged with apprehending loyalists in Bedminster Township.[18] But in early spring 1777, a smallpox epidemic broke out among Washington's troops in Morristown and ravaged the surrounding towns and countryside, including Bedminster. On March 26, King's son John died; four days later his son James followed.[19] On April 4, John, Sr., made his will, and

16. Somerset County Will no. 510.

17. Somerset County (NJ), Will no. 510; Lamington Presbyterian Church Session Minutes, Bedminster Township, 1749-1762, New Jersey State Archives, Trenton.

18. "Minutes of the Meetings of the Justices and Chosen Freeholders for the County of Somerset, 13 May 1772-2 September 1822," *Somerset County Historical Quarterly,* vol. 5, no. 4 (1916), 241-247.

19. Isabella King McLean may have named her sons John and James after her brothers or father. William McLean, Sr.'s will (Hunterdon County Will no. 2218) only names sons John and William. There is no definitive proof that William's and John's other brother was James, but circumstantial evidence makes a good case. There was a clear oral tradition among the grandchildren of the war generation that William McLean, Jr., had two brothers who served in the Revolution. Both John and a James McLean enlisted in the loyalist New Jersey Volunteers. In 1780, Ja___ McLean is listed as a taxpayer in Kingwood Township along with William McLean and John McLean. *Hunterdon County, New Jersey, Taxpayers, 1778-1797* (Miami Beach: T.L.C. Genealogy, 1990). The name James is used frequently

four days later, he, too, was dead.[20] Smallpox during the Revolution took many more lives than actual fighting with the British.[21]

By all standards, King was a gentleman. His estate inventory, beyond his slaves, listed 245 bushels of wheat and 40 acres of wheat and rie [rye] in the field. King's farms were part of the lucrative wheat growing economy. Wheat gave New Jersey the name "bread basket of the British Empire."[22] Wheat—and enough sons to cultivate it—was a measure of wealth. Vast quantities were taken to New Brunswick and Trenton and loaded on boats for easy transport to New York and Philadelphia.[23] Silver-hilted swords were part and parcel of the social rank of King's family.

We don't know the political leanings of King and his sons in Bedminster in the first year of the war, and smallpox took them in the spring of 1777, just as the screws were tightened on loyalists. In January 1777, Washington issued a proclamation from

by the Kings and the McLeans. "James" was the purported McLean immigrant ancestor from Scotland. Pruden, "McLean." William Jr.'s son Nicholas named a son James (after Nicholas's uncle?). As Egbert Bush noted in a *Hunterdon County Democrat* article on August 3, 1933, John Mclean named a son James (after his brother James?). James Mclean purchased land in Alexandria, New Jersey, next to Kingwood, in 1804. In 1790, a William McLean was a taxpayer in Alexandria, and John McLean's widow, Christina, lived in Alexandria when she died.

20. Scott, "Lamington Burying Ground Inscriptions," 132; Somerset County Wills, no. 510.

21. Elizabeth Fenn, *Pox Americana: The Great Smallpox Epidemic of 1775-1782* (New York: Hill & Wang, 2001), 9, 92-93; *Morristown: A History and Guide. Official National Park Handbook* (National Park Service, 1983), 36-38.

22. Larry Kidder, *A People Harassed and Exhausted: The Story of a New Jersey Militia Regiment in the American Revolution* (Larry Kidder, 2014), 19.

23. *New Jersey Gazette*, October 14, 1778, in Francis B. Lee, ed. *Documents Relating to the History of the State of New Jersey*, vol. II (1778) (Trenton: 1903), 14.

Figure 26. Wheat made New Jersey wealth. Silver spoon handle with wheat sheaf. Taylor and Hinsdale silversmiths, Newark, New Jersey, 1815.

Morristown notifying all suspected loyalists that "they must either take an oath of allegiance to the United States or admit they preferred the interest and allegiance of Great Britain . . . and withdraw within the enemy's lines."[24] In October 1777, the New Jersey Council of Safety apprehended King's son-in-law, William McLean, Sr., as a suspected loyalist. In February 1779, William paid the required 100 pounds recognizance bond to Governor Livingston for refusing to take the oath of allegiance to the State of New Jersey. Those who refused the oath were permitted to live in the state, if they posted a bond and promised to "keep the peace and be of good behavior toward all liege subjects of the State."[25]

John King's grandsons and beneficiaries, John and James McLean, like their father, William, Sr., switched sides during the war. They first enlisted with the patriots. John joined as a private

24. John T. Cunningham, "New Jersey: A Revolutionary State Divided Against Itself," in *Reports and Proceedings for 2007*, The Washington Association of New Jersey, 2008, 24.

25. Phyllis B. D'Autrechy, "What Choice?" in *Hunterdon County Historical Newsletter* (fall 1992): 652; Hunterdon County (NJ) Recognizance no. 2303; *Minutes of the Council of Safety of the State of New Jersey* (Jersey City: John H. Lyon, 1872), 156.

before 1778 in the Somerset County Militia. James entered as a private in April 1777 in Captain Daniel Piatt's Company of Continentals in Morris County, and then in July as a private in Captain Dallas's Company, Oliver Spencer's Regiment, Continental Army.[26]

But in April 1779, Trenton Justice of the Peace Rensselaer Williams ordered John McLean to appear at the next Court of Quarter Sessions to answer charges against him "for going over to the enemy." The court levied a recognizance bond of 500 pounds on John as "principal" and 250 pounds on his father William, Sr., as "surety." John failed to appear at the next court session in August, and the state ordered that his fine be paid by his father, unless he appeared at the next court."[27] John never showed up. Few loyalists risked their lives by answering court summons.[28] So between February 1779 and the end of the year, William McLean, Sr., owed total fines of 850 pounds, an immense sum, possibly his

---

26. John joined as a private before 1778 in the Somerset County Militia. James entered as a private in April 1777 in Captain Daniel Piatt's company of Continentals in Morris County, and then in July as a private in Captain Dallas's company, Oliver Spencer's regiment, Continental Army. John may have been living with his King relatives in Bedminster, Somerset County. See Stryker, *Official Register of the Officers and Men,* 682; John McClean, Somerset, Certificate No. 1211 for the depreciation of his continental pay in the Somerset County Militia, issued May 10, 1784, for 11 shillings, 5 pence, New Jersey State Archives, Trenton. James also may have been living in Somerset County. Captain Daniel Piatt was from Pluckemin in Bedminster, and died of pneumonia at Jockey Hollow in April 1780 after requisitioning food from Somerset County for the troops. See http://www.findagrave.com, Daniel Piatt; New Jersey State Archives MSS. NOS. 3772, 2240, 3776.

27. Hunterdon County Recognizance No. 2285; August Term Minutes, 1779, Minutes, Common Pleas 1773-1782, Vol. 12.

28. Dennis P. Ryan, *New Jersey's Loyalists* (Trenton: The New Jersey Historical Commission, 1975), 19.

net worth. William, Sr., eventually squared his accounts with son John when he left him five shillings in his will.[29]

John McLean did "go over to the enemy" for a while, joining the loyalist New Jersey Volunteers in 1778.[30] But by spring 1780, he was back in the Continental army as an Express Rider in Quartermaster Joseph Lewis's Department, stationed at Morristown. He served Quartermaster Lewis during the starving spring of 1780 for the troops camped at Jockey Hollow on the Wick farm.

James McLean had deserted the Continentals by August 22, 1778, when he was taken prisoner from the New Jersey Volunteers during patriot Major John Sullivan's raid on Staten Island. Exchanged back to the loyalists in a few months, he served to the end of the war as a private and corporal in the Fourth Battalion of the New Jersey Volunteers.[31] After the war, despite their loyalism, both John and James McLean returned to their homes in Hunterdon County to live. Like many sometime loyalists, they found acceptance back in their communities where bonds of family and friends were stronger than patriot antagonism.

---

29. Hunterdon County Will no. 2218.

30. In May 1778, John enlisted as a private in Captain Garrett Keating's company of the loyalist New Jersey Volunteers. He served in General Courtland Skinner's guard, but in April 1779, the loyalist roll listed him as "deserted" at Staten Island. Loyalist File, New Jersey State Archives, Trenton, Nos. 303, 305, 307, 309, 311; Muster Rolls of Captain Garret Keating's Company, First Battalion, New Jersey Volunteers, July 14, 1778, September 1778, October 21, 1778 (Photocopies of New Jersey Volunteers Muster Rolls from Canadian Archives provided to J. Lawrence Brasher by Theodore Brush); Brush, *The King's Men,* 79.

31. He served under Lieutenant Colonel Abraham Van Buskirk from Bergen County. Email message from Todd Braisted to J. Lawrence Brasher, February 24, 2015; Loyalist Files Nos. 811, 813, 819, 821, 823, 825, 829, 831, 1161, 1167, 1171, 1189, New Jersey State Archives, Trenton.

Figure 27. The Wick House at Jockey Hollow, Morristown.
John McLean helped provision the army nearby, spring 1780.
Silus Watters' cousin Major Joseph Bloomfield quartered in the
house in the winter of 1776-1777. The house saw the Pennsylvania
Line mutiny in January 1781, before the mutineers decamped to
Princeton and met with Captain James Moore. Wood block print
by unidentified National Recovery Administration artist, 1936.

Neither the Morgan nor the McLean in-laws of the Watters
provided plausible candidates for the sword. None of their JM
Revolutionary soldiers held rank that allowed an officer's sword.
And no records showed any personal associations between them
and Silus, John, or Peter Watters. What likely soldier did Silus
Watters know with the initials JM?

Early in my quest I discovered that Silus served at least twice
in the militia company of Princeton Militia Captain James
Moore. At the time, I mistakenly thought that Silus lived not in

Princeton but in Hopewell during the Revolution, and I found little about Silus's military record. He died before Revolutionary War service narratives were required by the pension act of 1832. I did not know who his friends and associates were before he moved to Lebanon in 1792.

In fall 2017 at the Firestone Library, Princeton University, I discovered James Moore's account book for his Princeton tannery business for the year 1800. It showed that Silus's brother Foster Watters bartered hides for finished leather with Moore. That new trail took me by surprise to Silus Watters as a tavern keeper in the neighborhood of Princeton. Captain James Moore was well known by patrons of that tavern and a lifelong acquaintance of Silus.

CHAPTER 5

Captain James Moore: "A Daring Officer (Late of Princeton)"

Barber and Howe, *Historical Collections of New Jersey*, 1844

He was regarded as a peculiarly skilful, brave, honest, and valuable officer . . . one of the best captains in New Jersey.

John Hulfish, 1833
Private in James Moore's Company, 1777-1778[1]

He always harassed his company by the repetition of his Revolutionary exploits.

George William Crump, 1833
Chief Clerk of the Federal Bureau of Pensions
Princeton, Class of 1805[2]

---

1. Revolutionary War Pension File W1060.

2. Pension File W1060

In the eighteenth century, "harass" meant "urge on" or "urge to attack." George William Crump, Chief of the Federal Bureau of Pensions, knew James Moore when Moore was in his fifties, while Crump was a student at Princeton in 1804-1805. Crump bears the distinction of being the first recorded streaker in the United States. Prior to Princeton, he attended Washington and Lee University (then Washington College) in Lexington, VA, where he was arrested by the authorities for running naked through the town. The embarrassed southern school suspended him for the remainder of the 1804 term, but only a month later Princeton happily enrolled him, and he graduated the following year.[3] Crump, the lusty student, and Moore, the doughty captain, exchanged lively stories of their personal and war time prowess.

In 1842, John Barber and Henry Howe traveled New Jersey transcribing oral history, interviewing "survivors of the Revolution . . . to rescue incidents which would otherwise be lost in the lapse of time." In their book *Historical Collections of the State of New Jersey* (1844), the story of James Moore's bold charge at Nassau Hall first saw print, related by his contemporaries, perhaps eyewitnesses of the event, twelve years after his death.[4]

Born May 5, 1751, in Hopewell, New Jersey, Moore grew up on the Scotch Road about five miles north of Trenton and two or three miles southwest of Pennington. James was only five years old, and one of eight children, when his father, Joseph Moore, Jr., died. Joseph bequeathed his widow, Helena, and their children a large wheat plantation lying on both sides of the Scotch Road

---

3. Pension File W1060; *University Chronology*, Washington and Lee, 2011, www.wlu.edu/about-wandl/history-and-traditions/a-brief-history/university-chronology.

4. Barber and Howe, *Historical Collections*, 3, 272-273.

with two houses and slaves. He also had employed indentured servants and owned a tannery.[5]

There were three branches of Moores in Hopewell, all of whom descended from The Rev. John Moore (1620-1657) of Ireland and his wife, Margaret Howell (1622-1670), whose families settled in Lynn, Massachusetts, in 1636. After John completed his studies at Harvard, in 1652, he and Margaret and thirty-five other families from Massachusetts purchased 12,000 acres from the Indians on Long Island and founded the village of Newtown. One grandson, Nathaniel, bought land in New Jersey and settled at what became Pennington. Another grandson, Gershom, moved to Maidenhead, now Lawrenceville, New Jersey. A third grandson, Joseph, bought a large tract along the Scotch Road near Birmingham, southwest of Pennington. He was James Moore's grandfather.

In December 1776, James's family met Washington leading his troops on the Scotch Road to the Battle of Trenton. At Birmingham, before dawn the day after Christmas, the noise of the soldiers passing by awakened the household of James's uncle Benjamin Moore. Benjamin and his wife brought out cider and mince pie, a traditional Christmas treat, which Washington and his immediate officers consumed on horseback, while they planned the imminent attack.[6]

---

5. James W. Moore, *Rev. John Moore of Newtown, Long Island, and Some of His Descendants* (Easton, PA: Chemical Publishing Co., 1903), 79-85; Hunterdon County Will No. 411.

6. James W. Moore, *Rev. John Moore*, 79-85; Letter from David Blackwell to J. Lawrence Brasher, December 14, 2017; John O. Raum, *History of the City of Trenton* (Trenton: W.T Nicholson and Co., 1871), 155.

James Moore and Silus Watters were born on May 5 and May 15 respectively in the same year, 1751, in the same community. They were friends from earliest childhood. The Moores and the Watters were related by blood or marriage to virtually all of the founding families of Hopewell Township. Both James and Silus counted relatives among the families of Armitage, Titus, Phillips, Hunt, Hart, Muirhead, Guild, Van Kirk, Burrowes, Scudder, Morgan, Woolsey, Mershon, Stout, and Savidge. Like other rural settlements in eighteenth-century New Jersey, Hopewell-Maidenhead was a kinship community. There were no strangers. The interlayering of making and trading in the self-provisioning farm economy was how people came to know each other. Exchanges formed friendships, courtships, and politics.[7]

James Moore and Silus Watters were cousins, at least by marriage, several times over. For instance, Joseph Moore of Pennington, cousin of James Moore's father, Joseph Moore, Jr., married Mary Armitage, who was a first cousin of Silus Watters' mother, Priscilla Titus Watters. The esteemed medical doctor in Hopewell, Benjamin Van Kirk, who dressed soldiers' wounds after the Battle of Princeton, married Silus's cousin Sarah Armitage, and treated the maladies of both the Moores and the Watters.[8] The extended families of James and Silus touched and interwove like roots and branches of trees in an old-growth forest.

Both families received spiritual nourishment from the Presbyterian Church at Pennington, where they had provided generations of leadership since its founding. James Moore's cousins

---

7. Bushman, *The American Farmer*, 36.

8. Benjamin VanKirk Medical Day Books, Hopewell Museum, Hopewell, NJ.

Nathaniel Moore (1687-1759) and Nathaniel's son Joseph (1721-1797) were trustees of the church. Silus Watters' maternal great-grandfather Enoch Armitage (1677-1739) and grandfather Ephraim Titus (1696-1789) were successive ruling elders. James and Silus, only ten days apart in age, grew up attending the same meeting house, singing hymns and listening to sermons together. And they would do so again as young men in the First Presbyterian Church of Princeton.

As a minor heir with five brothers ahead of him, James received no land and only 60 pounds in his father's will, half of the money to be paid him when he reached twenty-one.[9] Raised by his oldest brother, Joseph III, he may have been apprenticed at the tannery his father had owned. When he was twenty-one he left his brother's home and in 1773 purchased a house in Princeton from Richard Kinnan.[10] He lived there for sixty years.

He began operating his own tannery a year later. His house in the village stood on the north side of the King's Highway, now Nassau Street, near present day Moore Street, then about a quarter of a mile east of the college. James built his tannery behind and perhaps east of his house and east of the village. Tanneries emitted such a great stench that they preferably were located down-wind from settlements.

The tanning process was lengthy and complex. Tanners and farmers—the latter supplied the raw hides—usually divided the hides equally. The tanner returned half of the cured hides to the farmer and kept the other half to sell for profit. After a preliminary

---

9. James W. Moore, *Rev. John Moore*, 84; Hunterdon County Will No. 411.

10. Hageman, *Princeton*, I, 189; Somerset County Mortgage Book A, 364-365.

washing, hides were placed in sunken stone lime vats to burn the hair off. After the vats, the hides were de-limed by dumping a stinking assortment of urine, feces, or stale beer over them. One recipe recommended fourteen quarts of dog dung to be applied to every four dozen skins. The final stage was the tanning process in which washed hides were soaked in a tannin solution of ground tree bark and water. After tanning, the leather was curried with tallow to make it soft and pliable.[11]

In Moore's tannery account book for 1800-1801, Silus Watters' brother Foster, who lived near Silus's former Princeton tavern in Cherry Valley, made four deliveries of raw "hides and skins" between December and August for which Moore paid him tanned skins the following December. Robert Savidge, brother-in-law of Silus and Foster, in June 1801 paid Moore for "sundries." Their

Figure 28. Hides being put into lime vats. *Encyclopedia of Sciences, Arts and Trades*, Diderot, 1769.

---

11. "Tanning: A Colonial Trade," www.colonialsense.com.

attorney, Richard Stockton, Jr., was also a customer. Below Foster Watters' account Moore listed "Tulon, Frenchman," who loaned him cash in December 1800 and was paid back in tanned hides in December 1801. Louis Tulane ("Tulon") also had settled in Cherry Valley in 1791 after fleeing a slave insurrection in Haiti. His son Paul of Princeton and New Orleans, endowed Tulane University.[12] Moore supplied most of the leather in town.

James Moore was married twice. His first wife, Phebe, died at Princeton in 1791 when only thirty-six. Nothing is known about her. Her obituary simply stated that she "had long resided at that place."[13] James wasted no time, and eight months later he married Abigail Johnson of Newark.[14] "Much respected for her piety," "Abby" outlived James by fifteen years, dying in 1847.[15] James died childless in 1832, but two plain fieldstones near Phebe's grave may mark children who died as infants.[16]

Moore's tannery did well. He early speculated in land. In 1779, he bought a tract on the road to Kingston for 1476 pounds

---

12. "Moore Street Tanner Account Book, 1800-1801," 44-45, 63, 74, CO199 no. 701q, Rare Books and Special Collections, Firestone Library, Princeton University. Silus Watters moved away from Princeton in 1792. Since his brother Foster was a customer of Moore, Silus probably was also. Moore's account books from 1773-1796, cited in 1879 by Hageman, *Princeton*, I, 189, are no longer extant.

13. Thomas B. Wilson, "Notices from New Jersey Newspapers, 1781-1790, vol. 1 (Lambertville, New Jersey: Hunterdon House, 1988), 333, *Brunswick Gazette*, January 17, 1792.

14. Wilson, Vol. 3, 170, *Woods Newark Gazette*, August 16, 1792.

15. Hageman, *Princeton* I, 190.

16. "Burials in Princeton Cemetery," Genealogical Society of New Jersey, December 19, 1946, manuscript, courtesy Fred Sisser. The two plain stones were present in 1946.

from merchant Richard Patterson.[17] The year before, he purchased twelve acres in Princeton on the south side of the King's Highway from Moore Furman and Abraham Hunt, Trenton's leading mercantile partnership.[18] Moore Furman (1728-1808) was a cousin of James from Hopewell, a descendant of Gershom Moore. Like James and Silus, he was raised in the Presbyterian congregation at Pennington. Before the Revolution Furman gave the church an elegant marble top communion table.[19] His business

Figure 29. Moore Furman (1728-1808), High Sheriff of Hunterdon County, Deputy Quartermaster General of New Jersey for the Continental Army, cousin of James Moore. He freed his slaves in 1784.

partner, Abraham Hunt, entertained the unsuspecting Hessian Colonel Rahl in his cozy Trenton home on the night of Washington's crossing.

Furman was one of the wealthiest men in New Jersey. High Sheriff of Hunterdon County and postmaster of Trenton, who also had business interests in Philadelphia, in 1775, he was commissioned a captain in the Philadelphia Associators. He received appointment from George Washington in 1778 as Deputy Quartermaster General and Forage Master of New Jersey in charge of collecting and transporting all supplies to the Continental Army. An elder in the

17. A. Van Doren Honeyman, *Somerset County Historical Quarterly* (1912), 164.

18. Email from David Blackwell to J. Lawrence Brasher, December 16, 2017.

19. York, *The Pennington Area Presbyterians*, 74.

Presbyterian Church of Trenton, after the war Furman was one of the few who resolved the irony of winning liberty yet owning slaves. "Convinced of the iniquity and inhumanity of slavery," he freed his slaves as a New Year's resolve in 1784.[20] His anti-slavery stand may have induced his cousin James partially to follow suit. James Moore owned several slaves. In colonial New Jersey, slaves constituted between twelve and fifteen percent of the population of East Jersey. There were still over 7000 slaves in New Jersey in 1820.[21] Between 1813 and 1824, James Moore freed at least three slaves, but his will of 1828 still left to his wife, Abigail, "my mulatto boy John and my black girl Julia until by law they are entitled to their freedom."[22]

In 1833, John Hulfish and Princeton postmaster Stephen Morford were the only soldiers still alive who had served in James Moore's Revolutionary War militia company. Testifying on behalf of widow Abby Moore's pension application, Hulfish asserted that Moore "sustained immense losses in his private fortune by the depredations of the enemy and was reduced from

20. New Jersey Society of Colonial Dames of America, *The Letters of Moore Furman* (New York: F.H. Hitchcock, 1912), x.

21. Martha A. Sandweiss and Craig Hollander, "Princeton and Slavery: Holding the Center," www.slavery.princeton.edu/stories/princeton-and-slavery-holding-the-center.

22. *Somerset Historical Quarterly*, vol. 1(1912), "Record of Manumissions, 1805-1825," 276, 278-279; Somerset County Will No. 2443R. New Jersey's gradual emancipation law of 1804 required African Americans to serve lengthy apprenticeships until early adulthood for masters of their slave mothers.

affluence to poverty, a fact from which he never recovered."[23] The British ransacked everything in Princeton. Moore's tannery was stripped. Seeking post-war damage payment, Moore listed losses including "275 hides near tanned, 145 ½ hides part tanned, 4 dozen sheep skins, 17 cords bark, 10 sides of curried leather, 1 dozen curried calf skins—valued in all at 628 pounds." Besides his tannery stock, Moore lost such other goods as "a pleasure slay, 100 bushels of wheat and Indian corn, 8 tuns hay, sundry kinds china and earthenware, 200 pannels post and rail fence, 150 pannels worm fence"—all losses valued at 755 pounds, a huge sum. Historian Varnum Lansing Collins would write, "We can easily imagine with what grim energy [Moore] led the charge on Nassau Hall at the close of the battle . . . and demanded the surrender of the British soldiers still within the walls."[24] A few weeks before, the British also stole all the livestock, including a "yoke of fat oxen," from the farm of James's brother Joseph who raised him. In September 1780, James advertised for his missing sorrel mare with white mane and tail, perhaps then carrying a British rider.[25]

No one escaped the devastation in Princeton, "through and around which," Moore recalled, "the enemy so often passed and

---

23. Pension File W1060.

24. "Inventory of the Goods and Chattels of Capt. James Moore taken and destroyed by the British Army in December 1776 and January 1777," New Jersey Archives, Department of Defense Records, Revolutionary War Series No. 4288; Varnum Lansing Collins, ed., *A Brief Narrative of the Ravages of the British and Hessians at Princeton in 1776-1777* (Princeton: The University Library, 1906), 8.

25. "An inventory of the Cattle and Sheep taken from Joseph Moore, December 12, 1776, in James Moore, *Rev. John Moore*, 84; *New Jersey Gazette*, vol. III, no. 143, September 20, 1780, in William Nelson, *Documents Relating to the Revolutionary History of the State of New Jersey*, vol. IV, (Trenton: State Gazette Publishing Co.,1914), 42.

hovered, and which was so often the seat of war."[26] In contrast to some areas of New Jersey, relatively few loyalists inhabited the Princeton-Hopewell area.[27] Moore's militia served a defiantly patriotic community. His proximate relatives included multiple military officers. Among them, James's cousin Captain Jonathan Phillips (1738-1818) of Hopewell (also nephew of Silus Watters' Aunt Ruth Phillips) was an original member of the Society of the Cincinnati. James's cousin Captain Moses Moore (also cousin of Silus Watters) commanded a company of the Continental "Jersey Blues" and fought at the battles of Trenton, Princeton, and Monmouth.[28]

As a "skilful" captain who "harassed his troops," Moore and his men rattled the village with shouts of a marching chant reputedly composed by him that rhymed his resentment of England:

I love with all my heart
The independent part.

To obey the Parliament
My conscience won't consent.

I never can abide
To fight on England's side.

---

26. Pension File W1060.

27. About 8 percent of land in today's Princeton Township, 950 acres, were loyalist properties that were confiscated and sold, but some parcels were large tracts owned by one individual. Wanda S. Gunning, "The Town of Princeton and the University, 1756-1946," *The Princeton University Library Chronicle*, vol. 66, No. 3 (Spring 2005), 455.

28. Eli F. Cooley, *Genealogy of Early Settlers in Trenton and Ewing, New Jersey* (Trenton: M.S. Sharp Printing Co., 1883), 172-173.

I pray that God may bless
The great and grand Congress.

This is my mind and heart,
Though none should take my part.

The man that's called a Tory,
To plague, it is my glory,

Tho' righteous is the cause,
To keep the Congress laws.

To fight against the king
Bright liberty will bring.

Lord North and England's king,
I hope that they will swing.

Of this opinion I
Resolve to live and die.[29]

---

29. Hageman, *Princeton*, I, 189, says that this "expression of [Moore's] patriotic sentiments" was found among Moore's papers in his own handwriting. The
book *Patriotic Poems of New Jersey* edited by William Clinton Armstrong (Newark: New Jersey Society of Sons of the American Revolution, 1906), 3, titles the
rhyme "The Jerseyman's Resolve" and claims that it was "a marching chant of
the New Jersey militia, 1776," composed by James Moore. The rhyme appears to
have been widely known in the colonies. *Bob Taylor's Magazine*, vols. 11-12 (Taylor's Publishing Co., 1910), 472, states that it appeared in manuscript in 1782 in
Robert Carter's Nomini Hall, Westmoreland County, VA, letter book. Its appear-
ance in Carter's hand is particularly interesting because Princeton graduate Philip
Vickers Fithian was a tutor at Nomini Hall in 1773-1774 and having heard the
chant in Princeton very likely recited Moore's rhyme to Carter. Wilfred Harold
Monro in *The History of Bristol, Rhode Island* (J.A. and R.A. Reid, 1881), 175,
states that the rhyme was found in the handwriting of Captain Simeon Potter
(1720-1806) of Bristol, RI.

The First Presbyterian Church, later named Nassau Presbyterian, also prayed and preached Moore's marching plea for God to bless the Congress. A hotbed of patriots, in 1772, the year Moore moved to Princeton, the church experienced a revival under the exhortations of The Reverend Doctor John Witherspoon that drew newcomer Moore and other young people into the congregation.[30]

A brick Georgian structure constructed on college land in 1762, the church served Princeton until it was ransacked by the British in December 1776. It reopened in 1784. The "audience room" contained a three-sided gallery, where all slaves and free blacks were required to sit apart from the congregation downstairs. Part of the balcony also was designated for college students, and the college reserved the right to use the church for commencement ceremonies and guest speakers. The elevated pulpit perched high on the middle of a side wall of the rectangular room. It was topped after the post-war refurbishing with a sounding board festooned with curtains fastened by a large gilded star. Fifty-seven box pews on the main floor were rented by prominent members. Twenty-three square pew compartments, slightly raised and more expensive, lined the walls, while thirty-four narrower rectangular ones filled the center. Moore paid fifteen pounds for his square box on the back wall facing the pulpit.

On Sundays his gaze tallied his connections to an extraordinary patriot company unmatched in revolutionary zeal by any other New Jersey congregation and where the cords of family and

---

30. Hageman, *Princeton*, II, 86.

Figure 30. Seal of the Nassau Presbyterian Church, Princeton.
The only surviving depiction of the original meetinghouse
(1766-1813), where James Moore and his Revolutionary cohort
worshipped. COURTESY OF NASSAU PRESBYTERIAN CHURCH, PRINCETON.

friends thickly interwove those of faith.[31] Two signers of the Declaration of Independence were present—The Reverend Dr. John
Witherspoon, "an ecclesiastic with lance in hand" and the only
cleric to sign the Declaration, and attorney Richard Stockton.[32]
The aristocratic Stocktons worshipped in the square pew visible
to all in the front right corner. Richard, a trustee of the college,

---

31. The description of the congregation is in part from a plan of the rented
pews recorded probably between the restoration of the church in 1784 and 1796,
the year that Samuel Stout, Jr., who is listed, died. Hageman, *Princeton*, II, 82
overleaf. The earliest extant list of "communicants" is from 1792, the year Silus
Watters moved away from Princeton.

32. The metaphor describing Witherspoon is from Hageman, *Princeton*, I, 96.

informal pre-war ambassador to England, and master of the elegant family estate, Morven, was with his wife, Annis, a long-time friend of George and Martha Washington. Annis Boudinot Stockton was one of America's first published female poets. Her brother Elias Boudinot was President of the Continental Congress. The Stocktons' Philadelphia son-in-law and frequent visitor, Dr. Benjamin Rush, also signed the Declaration. Among the Stockton children in the pew was their eldest son, Richard, Jr., who at age twelve remained behind to watch over the already ransacked Morven during the Battle of Princeton, while his parents fled into hiding. Later known as "Duke" Stockton, he, too, became a lawyer, the most eminent in New Jersey, and a United States Senator. In 1807, Silus Watters retained Richard, Jr., and his office partner, Thomas Johnson, as counsel in a contest over the estate of Silus's Princeton father-in-law, William Savidge. Johnson lived on the corner opposite James Moore in the village.[33]

To Moore's right and forward two and three pews sat the Beattys. Physician Dr. John Beatty (1749-1821), a Princeton graduate and son of the renowned preacher Charles Beatty and his wife, Ann Reading Beatty, rose to the rank of major in the Continental Army. Captured with his brother Reading Beatty (1757-1831) in the calamitous defeat of Fort Washington, he suffered a two-year brutal captivity on a British prison ship. After his exchange, he served as Commissary General for Prisoners and as a delegate to the Continental Congress. He was a charter member of the Society of the Cincinnati. John Beatty's brother "Arky"—his parents

---

33. "Receipt of Silas Watters, administrator of William Savage, a retaining fee in the dispute of a pretended will and counsel fee to attend the Somerset Court as counsel in support of the case." Signed, Richard Stockton, December 1807, Watters Papers.

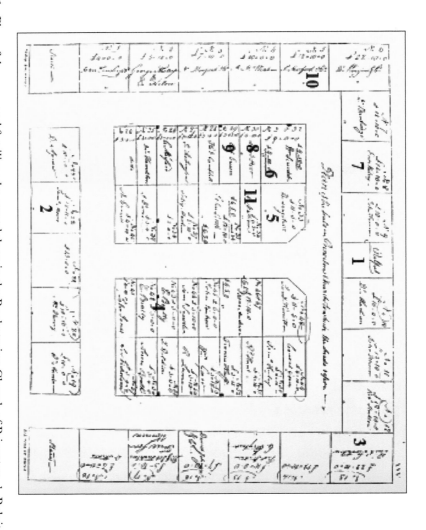

Figure 31. Plan of the pews and families who rented them in the Presbyterian Church of Princeton. 1. Pulpit, 2. James Moore, 3. Stockton, 4. Beatty, 5. Longstreet, 6. Scudder, 7. Kelsey, 8. Stout, 9. Cruser, 10. Morford, 11. Mattison.

surprised by his birth late in their marriage invented his name, "Erkuries," which in Greek means "from the Lord"—at age sixteen helped capture a British transport as a member of a privateer crew out of Elizabethtown. In 1775, colonial legislatures authorized attacks on enemy cargoes by private ship owners. Whalers, fishermen, teachers, and preachers signed on, ready to make a quick fortune. American privateers captured over 3,000 ships during the war.[34] A military adventurer, Arky was a ladies' man who did not marry until he was forty. After a wartime assignment at York, Pennsylvania, in a single letter to his brother Reading Beatty, he detailed the individual charms and flaws of no less than seventeen young eligible women of the town.[35]

Erkuries Beatty was a captain in the Continental army and was wounded at the Battle of Germantown, where Moore also fought. He survived five major battles and saw the British surrender at Yorktown. He, too, joined the Society of the Cincinnati and later served as mayor of Princeton.

Figure 32. Erkuries Beatty (1759-1823)

John and Arky's sister Elizabeth ("Betsy") Beatty married the young Presbyterian minister Philip Vickers Fithian (1747-1776) of Greenwich, New Jersey. Close in age, James Moore knew

---

34. Rick Atkinson, *The British Are Coming*, 468.

35. Erkuries Beatty to Reading Beatty, August 19, 1781, in Joseph M. Beatty, "Letters of the Four Beatty Brothers of the Continental Army, 1774-1794," *Pennsylvania Magazine of History and Biography*, 44 (1920), 222-226.

Fithian in 1776 when Philip volunteered as chaplain of General Nathaniel Heard's militia brigade in which Moore served. Fithian was with Heard at the Battle of Long Island, in the retreat back over the East River to New York City, and at the Battle of White Plains, New York. A 1772 graduate of the college, a favorite of President Witherspoon, and always at his sermons on Sundays, Fithian delivered the college commencement address on the topic "Political jealousy is a laudable passion." Two years later he joined with friends who burned British tea seized from a ship docked at his hometown on the lower Delaware River—the Greenwich Tea Party. On his visits courting Betsy Beatty in Princeton in 1775, Fithian was excited to see the militia drilling in the streets.[36]

Figure 33. Philip Vickers Fithian (1747-1776)

As a youth in Greenwich, New Jersey, Philip Fithian studied for the ministry at nearby Deerfield Academy in classes alongside future Revolutionary leader and New Jersey governor Joseph Bloomfield who was preparing for law. The Rev. Enoch Green was head of the academy—and Fithian's future brother-in-law. Green had married Betsy Beatty's older sister, Mary, in 1770, and

---

36. Robert Albion and Leonidas Dodson, eds., *Philip Vickers Fithian: Journal: 1775-1776* (Princeton: Princeton University Press, 1934), 131. Silas Deane on his way to the Continental Congress in early May 1775 wrote his wife that a militia escorted him to Princeton . . . "where we were received by a company under arms." *The Deane Papers*, Collections of the New York Historical Society (New York, 1887-1901), I, 226-227.

Fithian met Betsy at Green's house. A valedictorian 1760 Princeton graduate, Enoch Green was a cousin of both Joseph Bloomfield and Silus Watters. All three were descendants of Enoch Armitage (1677-1739), the first elder of the Pennington Presbyterian Church.[37]

The brothers-in-law Philip Fithian and Enoch Green were early casualties of the war. As chaplain of Heard's brigade, Fithian died of "camp fever" (dysentery) on October 22, 1776, near Fort Washington in Manhattan. His widow, Betsy, returned home to Princeton to live with her brother John Beatty and sister-in-law Mary Longstreet Beatty and sought spiritual solace from Dr. Witherspoon, her late husband's mentor.[38] Six weeks after Philip Fithian's death, his brother-in-law Enoch Green also died of dysentery as a chaplain in the Continental Army. Two months more and the twenty-one-year-old brother-in-law of Philip and Enoch, Charles Beatty, a lieutenant in the Continental Army, also suffered an untimely death. He had just purchased a "very handsome rifle." One of his friends in the ranks pointed it at Charles in jest saying, "Beatty, I will shoot you," and pulled the trigger. He did not know the gun was loaded, and Charles fell dead shot in the chest.[39]

---

37. York, *The Pennington Area Presbyterians*, 4, 21. Joseph Bloomfield's friends and associates burned the tea at Greenwich. He knew them from his student days at Deerfield Academy. Bloomfield served as counsel for their defense in their trial, and the patriot jury threw out the case. Mark Edward Lender and James Kirby Martin, *Citizen Soldier, The Revolutionary War Journal of Joseph Bloomfield* (Newark: New Jersey Historical Society, 1982), 3-4.

38. John Fea, *The Way of Improvement Leads Home, Philip Vickers Fithian and the Rural Enlightenment in Early America* (Philadelphia: University of Pennsylvania Press, 2008), 210.

39. Charles Clinton Beatty, Jr., https://www.wikitree.com/wiki/Beatty-2225.

The Beattys were bereft. Their grief was augmented and shared by their in-laws, the Longstreets, who sat in the double front pew on the left facing the pulpit. The senior Richard Longstreet had subscribed for the building of the church in 1762 and was later ruling elder. He and his wife, Margaret Cowenhoven Longstreet, had two sons, Richard, Jr., and Aaron, a captain of the Princeton militia, and two daughters, Mary and Eleanor. Their daughter Mary was John Beatty's wife. While retreating from the British near Morristown, perhaps on one of the early Forage War raids that Washington encouraged, Richard, Jr., was killed by a British ball.

In the space of four months, the Beattys and the Longstreets together mourned the deaths of four young family members: Philip Fithian, Enoch Green, Charles Beatty, and Richard Longstreet, Jr. Other calamities visited the related Scudder family in the pew adjacent to the Longstreets. In December 1776, William and Lemuel Scudder—Lemuel served in Moore's company—brothers-in-law of John Beatty and Aaron Longstreet, endured the British destruction of their mills at Princeton and Kingston and the burning of William's house.[40] "O Doleful! Doleful! Doleful!—Blood! Carnage! Fire!!," wrote Philip Fithian after

---

40. William Scudder (1731-1793) married Sarah Van Dyke, sister of Anna Van Dyke who married Aaron Longstreet. Lemuel Scudder (1741-1806) married Eleanor Longstreet, sister of Aaron Longstreet and Mary Longstreet Beatty. See Rubert James Longstreet, "A Longstreet Family History," (DeLand, Florida, 1960), http://sites.rootsweb.com/~longstrt/history.html; Hageman, Princeton, I, 56; Creesy, Virginia Keys, "The Battle of Princeton," *Princeton Alumni Weekly*, 77, No. 11 (December 6, 1976), 12-20; Pay Roll of Capt. James Moore's Company, Second Battalion of Col. VanDykes "as a guard at this place and guarding prisoners at Head Quarters, Princeton, May 24-June 4, 1778," New Jersey State Archives.

witnessing the Battle of Long Island in September 1776. His words portended not only his early personal fate but also that of the young Beattys, Longstreets, and Scudders.[41]

James Moore felt closely the interfamilial grief upon grief of the Beattys, Longstreets, and Scudders. Near the start of his military service and through all of these dire losses, James served as lieutenant under Captain Aaron Longstreet. Moore took over as captain from Longstreet in March 1777, when Aaron resigned in the midst of his extended family's suffering.[42]

William Churchill Houston preceded Aaron Longstreet as James Moore's militia captain in 1776. From North Carolina, Houston was a student prodigy, protégé and close friend of Dr. Witherspoon. A 1768 graduate of the college, he was appointed Professor of Mathematics and Natural Philosophy in 1771. He

Figure 34. William Churchill Houston (1746-1788) by Archibald Robertson.

---

41. Albion and Dodson, *Philip Fithian*, 218.

42. Affidavit of Stephen Morford, Pension File W1060. Richard Longstreet, Sr., and his son Aaron lived in the still extant "gentleman's country seat," "Maybury Hill" about two miles northeast of the college. In 1783 Richard and Aaron were farming more than 550 acres. Aaron was a blacksmith and one of the owners of the "New Waggon" stage line between Princeton and Philadelphia. Aaron Longstreet (born ca. 1750) of Princeton, son of Richard (1718-1795), is not to be confused with Aaron Longstreet, Jr., (1741-1829) of New Brunswick, son of Aurie Longestrat (1710-1793), also a captain in the Middlesex County, New Jersey, militia. *Princeton Recollector*, Vol. 8, No. 8, September 1, 1983; Longstreet, "A Longstreet Family History."

never missed Sunday worship until the British occupied and ransacked the church in December 1776. At the college, he was in charge of the celebrated orrery, an apparatus showing the position and motion of the bodies of the solar system, purchased by Witherspoon and made by Philadelphia inventor David Rittenhouse.

Houston served as captain of the Somerset militia in the Princeton area beginning in February 1776. He returned to teach at the college in August, but re-enlisted in the militia in November for four months, when the British forces entered Princeton and the college closed. He led actions and scouting expeditions in the vicinity of Princeton. A member of the New Jersey Provincial Congress in 1776, he was elected Deputy Secretary of the Continental Congress in 1777 and was a delegate from 1779-1781. Moving to Trenton in 1782, he became a leader in the Trenton Presbyterian Church. He studied law with Richard Stockton, Jr., set up a practice in Trenton in 1785, and took interest in Trenton silversmith John Fitch's effort to build a steamboat on the Delaware. He was elected to the Constitutional Convention in 1787 but died of tuberculosis before he could attend. James Moore, Aaron Longstreet, Silus Watters' brother Foster, and probably Silus Watters himself served together under Captain Houston in the Somerset militia in 1776.[43]

Enos Kelsey sat in a square pew to the left of the pulpit on the wall opposite Moore. A merchant whose store faced the college, Enos was a member of the Provincial Congress in 1775 and Deputy Quartermaster for Clothing for the New Jersey Continental

---

43. James McLachan, ed., *Princetonians, 1748-1768, A Biographical Dictionary* (Princeton: Princeton University Press, 1976), 643-647; Thomas Allen Glenn, *William Churchill Houston, 1746-1788* (Norristown, PA: Privately Printed, 1903), 19-21; Foster Watters, Revolutionary Pension File 11100.

line. English born attorney Jonathan Deare, who married Frances Phillips, a distant cousin of Silus Watters, attended the church. With Kelsey he represented Princeton in the Provincial Congress in 1775. In 1780 he chaired the Association to Prevent Trade with the Enemy. James Moore and John Witherspoon were members of his committee.[44]

Seven pews in front of Moore, under the rays of the radiant star above Witherspoon's pulpit, sat silversmith Samuel Stout, Jr., and his wife, Helena Cruser Stout. He was the only permanently established silversmith in Princeton. His shop did business near the corner of Nassau and Witherspoon streets. Samuel's father-in-law, Abraham Cruser, kept an eye on his grandchildren from the pew behind. Samuel Stout, Silus Watters, and Silus's brothers-in-law William Savidge, Jr., and Daniel Leigh, served as friends together in Moore's Company at Springfield just prior to the battle there in June 1780. They slept on their guns in the fields along the Rahway River by order of Baron Von Steuben.[45]

Friends and families in the pews mirrored home neighborhoods. The Stouts, Watters, Savidges, and Crusers lived within a mile or so of each other where the Rocky Hill-Pennington Road crossed the Province Line in northwest Princeton. While no communicant lists of the Princeton church survive before 1792, the year Silus Watters moved away to Lebanon, he and his in-laws, the Savidges, would have attended the Princeton church. And not all members and attenders purchased pews. Raised with James Moore in the Pennington Presbyterian Church, Silus Watters was

---

44. Hageman, Princeton, I, 72-73.

45. Testimony of John Hulfish, Revolutionary Pension File W1060.

an ardent birthright Presbyterian.[46] When he moved to Princeton, he lived much closer to the Presbyterian congregation there than to the one in Pennington, and many of his friends and patrons of his tavern were staunch members at Princeton. His sister Mary Watters Savidge was a communicant of the Princeton church prior to her removal to Basking Ridge.[47] Her husband, William Savidge, Jr., Silus's militia compatriot at Springfield, was Silus's double brother-in-law. William also was the brother of Silus's wife, Sarah Savidge Watters. When William and Mary Watters Savidge moved to Basking Ridge, they joined the Presbyterian congregation there and were buried near the ancient white oak whose limbs spread over the churchyard and under which George Whitefield had preached in 1740. In the eighteenth century, steadfast denominational loyalties governed which church one attended. Silus Watters and James Moore worshipped together among the Princeton Presbyterian patriots.[48]

Moore nodded his greetings to Stephen Morford, who with his wife, Mary Hamilton Morford, occupied a square pew toward the front on the left wall. Morford, who also later testified on behalf of widow Abby Moore's pension application in 1833, served in the militia under Moore from December 1776 until the end of the war. Under Moore's command, Morford guarded British

46. Silus Watters later was a founding member of the Pleasant Grove Presbyterian Church near his home in Lebanon.

47. Undated Communicant Roll from Records of the Presbyterian Church of Princeton, New Jersey State Archives, Trenton, New Jersey.

48. From before the Revolution, men in my Watters family line married only Presbyterian women for five generations. My grandfather Lawrence Watters still attended a Presbyterian church after he married, preferring it to my grandmother's Methodist church.

prisoners in Nassau Hall after the Battle of Princeton, and later with Moore marched prisoners from the Battle of Monmouth to Philadelphia. Stephen Morford and his family were postmasters at Princeton for thirty years at the corner of Nassau and Witherspoon streets.[49]

Next to Samuel Stout, Jr., in the twin pew on his right sat the family of Aaron and Sarah Cooke Mattison. Both Aaron Mattison and Stephen Morford were friends and near neighbors of Samuel Stout in the village center. The two took the inventory of Samuel Stout's estate, including his silversmith tools, when he died early at age thirty-nine from lingering effects of his 1776 imprisonment by the British in New York.[50] Beginning in 1776, Aaron Mattison was the Steward of Nassau Hall. The main task of the Steward was to maintain the college dining hall, but it included other duties of "collecting bills, tuition, fees, and room and pew rents [in the Presbyterian Church]. The Steward also sold textbooks, cleaned chimneys, guarded the belfry and bell-rope, hired and fired servants, and purchased college furniture." The position held such influence that Varnum Lansing Collins would write that "next to the President, [the Steward] was the chief executive of the college."[51]

Overseeing all aspects of Nassau Hall, Mattison perhaps witnessed with mixed feelings Moore and his friends breaking open

---

49. "Stephen Morford," www.ancestry.com/boards/surnames.morford/140/mb.ashx; Pension File W1060.

50. Inventory of the Goods and Chattels of Samuel Stout, Jr., late of Princeton, made May 27, 1795, New Jersey State Archives, Trenton.

51. "Steward and Refectory Records," AC032, Rare Books and Special Collections, Princeton University Library.

the front door to demand the surrender of the British. Mattison and Morford must have deliberated with Moore when managing the British prisoners later held by Moore inside the building after the battle. When it became a military hospital, Mattison was the coffin maker. Mattison also was a friend and patron of Silus Watters. He frequented Silus's tavern, attended Christmas parties there, and signed a required yearly petition vouching that Silus was "a proper person to keep a tavern."[52]

The gold-rayed star above the pulpit was not the brightest ornament in the audience room. The Reverend Doctor John Witherspoon (1723-1794), who preached beneath it and led the congregation throughout the revolutionary period, outshone it. A graduate of the University of Edinburgh, Witherspoon was urged by Richard Stockton, Stockton's son-in-law, Benjamin Rush, and English evangelist George Whitefield to leave Scotland for the presidency of the college at Princeton. In 1768 Witherspoon arrived at Princeton to become the sixth president of the college and minister of its Presbyterian Church. John Adams, who usually was suspicious of the role of clergy in politics, in 1774 called Witherspoon "as high

Figure 35. John Witherspoon (1723-1794) after Charles Willson Peale.

---

52. Silas Watters, Tavern Application, 1788. Biographical sketches of many of the communicants of the Presbyterian Church cited above may be found in Hageman, *Princeton*, I, 65-97.

a Son of Liberty as any Man in America."[53] In the pulpit, his Scottish burr made him difficult to understand, yet his powerful personality—in the eighteenth century called "presence"—affected all who heard him.

John Witherspoon rose quickly as one of the foremost revolutionary leaders not only in New Jersey but in all America. His overlapping activities in religion, education, and politics were unmatched. He encouraged patriotic orations at the college commencements. Off campus he chaired the Somerset County Committee of Correspondence and was a member of the New Jersey Provincial Congress. A delegate to the Continental Congress from 1776 to 1782, he authored one third of its religious proclamations—expressions of the theological-political grounding of the Revolution that asserted the providential care of the Almighty for the United States.[54] His former Edinburgh classmate, Adam Ferguson, British Commissioner to the Colonies in 1778, wrote a letter that year in which he trembled at the cunning of Adams, Franklin, and the "150,000 against us with Johnny Witherspoon at their head."[55] Jeffrey Morrison in

---

53. John Adams, diary entry of August 27, 1774, in *The Diary and Autobiography of John Adams,* ed. L.H. Butterfield, 4 vols. (Cambridge, MA: Harvard University Press, 1961), 2: 112.

54. Mark A. Noll, *Princeton and the Republic, 1768-1822* (Princeton: Princeton University Press, 1989), 28; Jeffrey H. Morrison, *John Witherspoon and the Founding of the American Republic* (Notre Dame, IN: University of Notre Dame Press, 2005), 77; Sheldon S. Cohen and Larry R. Gerlach, "Princeton in the Coming of the American Revolution," *New Jersey History,* vol. XCII (Summer 1974), 90-91.

55. Varnum Lansing Collins, *President Witherspoon* (Princeton University, 1925), vol. II, 35.

his biography of Witherspoon would call him "the New Jersey colossus."[56] John Witherspoon was the patriot pulpit giant who preached to James Moore and Silus Watters every Sunday.

———

In his pension affidavit of August 1832, three months before his death, James Moore summarized his participation in the Revolution: "From the time he first entered the service, he abandoned all personal and private business and devoted himself to the cause of his country in whatever way his services were required. He was almost without interruption employed in . . . taking care of provisions, stores, magazines, out on skirmishes, guarding the lines. Always when in Princeton, his whole time was employed in performing some duty for his country. He was in the service of his country from December 1775 until the close of the war."[57] The rest of Moore's narrative sketches only a bare bones outline of the times and places that he served and the names of his officers. His statement seems deliberately devoid of color, detail, and anecdote. The intrepid "exploits" by which he formerly "harassed" his militia cohorts appear nowhere in his account. By 1832 in great old age, Moore was infirm, blind for several years, and led about town by a boy.[58]

Moore first enlisted for a month in December 1775 as a private in Captain Gordon's company in the regiment of Nathaniel Heard. Moore and his cohorts spent their first Christmas of the war on Long Island "disarming Tories." He recalled that in

---

56. Morrison, *John Witherspoon*, 17.

57. Pension File W1060.

58. Hageman, *Princeton*, I, 190.

January 1776 he began serving as lieutenant in Princeton Captain Aaron Longstreet's company in the regiment of Colonel Henry Van Dyke, and he served under Van Dyke for the rest of the war.

Although Moore remembered that he was with Longstreet for 1776 and early 1777, he must have served first under Captain William Houston. Militia companies in December 1776 and January 1777 were in disarray. Checking on their farms and families, militiamen joined whomever they could in makeshift companies and came and went according to personal necessities. In the first half of 1776, Aaron Longstreet served not as captain but as lieutenant in Captain William Churchill Houston's company. On February 28, 1776, the Council of Safety ordered the creation of a Second Regiment of Foot militia in Somerset under the command of Colonel Abraham Quick, Esq., with William Houston as captain, Aaron Longstreet as first lieutenant, and James Stockton as ensign, a position Stockton kept under ensuing captains Longstreet and Moore.[59] After Houston resigned in August 1776 to return to teach at the college, Aaron Longstreet became captain and James Moore first lieutenant. When Longstreet resigned in March 1777, Moore then officially took over as captain under Colonel Henry Van Dyke.

---

59. Glenn, *Houston*, 19-20. Larry Kidder states, "So many records did not survive it is impossible to accurately trace all changes in company officer structure. Pension application statements are routinely full of errors as to commander because it kept changing so much that it was almost impossible to remember who was in command at what time." In December 1776 and January 1777, Longstreet's Princeton militia company was mixed with part of an Amwell company in a makeshift unit that was with Washington's army in Bucks County, Pennsylvania. Email from Larry Kidder to J. Lawrence Brasher, January 25, 2020.

James Moore's serving in 1776 in Captain Houston's company reveals another connection to the brothers Foster and Silus Watters. In his 1832 pension application, Foster Watters stated, "He served as a private under Col. Quick and Capt. Houston. At the time he entered service he resided near the town of Princeton and thinks it was in the year 1776. He was called out on every alarm. He first went to New York when the British fleet hove in sight at the Hook and remained there between one and two weeks under the command of Captain Houston and was sent back to his home near Princeton."[60] Foster's brother Silus died in 1820, so he left no application narrative for the pension act of 1832. In 1776, Foster was twenty-seven and Silus was twenty-five, so it is likely that they both served in Captain Houston's company side by side with James Moore.

William Houston, James Moore, and Foster and Silus Watters would have attended the celebration of American Independence in front of Nassau Hall on July 9, 1776. A crowd assembled to hear read a freshly printed copy of the Declaration of Independence. A witness wrote that Nassau Hall "was grandly illuminated and INDEPENDENCY proclaimed under a triple volley of musketry and universal acclamation for the prosperity of the UNITED STATES. The ceremony was conducted with the greatest decorum."[61] James Moore would have dressed for the occasion with his dog-head sword.

After the Battle of Long Island in August 1776 and the British occupation of New York and Staten Island, James Moore

---

60. Pension File 11100.

61. Extract of a letter from Princeton, dated July 10, 1776. *Pennsylvania Packet*, July 15, 1776.

"guarded the lines" at Amboy, Elizabethtown, and Newark. Whenever Aaron Longstreet was absent, Moore commanded the company. He was at Newark in November 1776 when Fort Washington fell in Manhattan, and in December he and his company met Washington's army at Newark and joined them in the retreat across New Jersey. Thomas Paine was traveling with the army, and, according to his own account, at that moment in Newark he penned the first words of *The American Crisis*, an opening sentence that "had the cadence of a drumbeat": "These are the times that try men's souls. The summer soldier and the sunshine patriot will, in this crisis shrink from the service of his country; but he that stands it now deserves the thanks of man and woman." *The Crisis* was read in the camps of the soldiers along the Delaware before the Battle of Trenton. Later they would repeat the first sentence as a watchword and a battle cry. Paine's words were the ballast that steadied the boats of Washington's crossing.[62]

James Moore crossed the Delaware River to Pennsylvania the day after Washington did. But "a few days before the Battle of Trenton," he stated, "some duty not now recalled called him to Princeton." In spite of his claim that as a soldier "he abandoned all personal and private business," Moore may have returned to Princeton before the Battle of Trenton to check on his pillaged tannery. With the British in Princeton, however, he could travel there only as a furtive scout. As a known patriot and officer in the militia he was a marked man. After Washington crossed the river to Pennsylvania, Houston's company and numerous other

---

62. New York *Public Advertiser*, August 22, 1807; Fischer, *Washington's Crossing*, 140, 142.

scouts continually returned to the Jersey side to spy on the British.[63] Silus Watters' cousin John Phillips "frequently crossed the Delaware on scouting parties to harass and alarm the enemy's pickets at Trenton."[64] Private James Agin "continued with his company as a scouting party crossing and re-crossing the river until the Battle of Princeton."[65] Colonel Joseph Reed's mounted scouts the day before the Battle of Princeton confirmed that there were no British sentries on the east side of town.[66] North of the village, adjacent to the homes of Silus and Foster Watters, the dissected and wooded Princeton Ridge or "Rocky Hill Mountain" that extended westward from the Millstone River into Hopewell provided hideouts for patriot scouts[67]

As lieutenant, James Moore likely accompanied his captain, Aaron Longstreet, on a noteworthy scouting "party" at Mapleton just east of Princeton. Longstreet's wife, Anna, was the daughter of Matthias and Eleanor Lane Van Dyke, prosperous farmers at Mapleton whose elegant stone "mansion" still stands.[68] Not long before the Battle of Princeton, the Van Dyke house was occupied by several British officers who demanded the Van Dykes prepare

---

63. Glenn, *Houston*, 24.

64. Pension File W575.

65. Pension File S2029

66. American Battlefield Trust, "Battle of Princeton," https://www.battlefields .org/learn/articles/10-facts-battle-princeton.

67. For instance, the wooded slopes of the ridge in contrast to the majority cultivated land in Somerset in the late eighteenth century is seen in a deed of Caesar Trent, an African-born free black, who owned a woodlot on Princeton Ridge. Much of the ridge was too steep and rough for farming. Gunning, "The town of Princeton," 462.

68. Aaron Longstreet married Anna Van Dyke September 11, 1763.

Figure 36. The Matthias and Eleanor Lane Van Dyke house at Mapleton, where Captain Longstreet captured the turkey dinner.

a roast turkey dinner to be ready for them when they returned "after routing rebels under Mr. Washington." Longstreet and his scouting company arrived from the Delaware at his in-laws' house just in time to eat the feast before the enemy guests returned. In later years, Longstreet "often related the capture of the roast turkey dinner with great satisfaction."[69] If Moore accompanied Captain Longstreet at the capture of the turkey, he was conveniently situated near Princeton to assist at Nassau Hall at the end of the battle.

James Moore spent most of the war leading scouting parties to protect New Jersey from marauding and foraging British troops. He was at the large-scale battles of Princeton and Germantown. And he performed other critical actions in major events of the war—protecting ammunition from the mutinous men of the

---

69. William B. Aitken, *Distinguished Families in America Descended from Wilhelmus Beekman and Jan Thomasse Van Dyke* (New York: The Knickerbocker Press, 1912), 221-224; Hageman, *Princeton*, I, 194-195.

Pennsylvania Line from Jockey Hollow, Morristown, while they camped at Princeton; guarding and transporting prisoners from the Battle of Monmouth; preparing for the Battle of Springfield under Baron Von Steuben. But Moore served most of the time "constantly on the lines to prevent plundering and excursions of the enemy" and to attack them at opportune times.[70] These continual forays would become known as the Forage Wars.

The normal war in New Jersey was a daily routine of fatigue and foraging punctuated by what the British called the *petite guerre*, or 'little war,' in which the militia fought with roving parties of regulars and Hessians.[71] The British from New York continually foraged for food, fodder, and firewood. Moore's militia skirmished with pillagers, kept roads passable, guarded prisoners and magazines, hunted down thieves, and monitored loyalists. The land near the Hudson River, called the "Neutral Ground," was a "no-man's land of ambush, robbery, burnings, murder, and the ubiquitous 'London Trade' of secretly supplying the British troops in New York with provisions."[72] Moore was there in Newark when Washington passed through in retreat. Besides Newark, Moore specifically recalled guarding the lines at Middlebrook under General Sullivan "while the main Army was stationed there and the British lay at Brunswick," at Amboy, Elizabethtown, New Brunswick, Pompton, Bergen, Somerset Court House, and continually along the Millstone River.[73]

---

70. Pension File W1060. The Pennsylvania Line occupied Princeton January 3-12, 1781.

71. Fischer, *Washington's Crossing*, 348.

72. "The Militia in New Jersey during the Revolution," www.doublegv.com /ggv/militia.html.

73. Pension File W1060.

James Moore likely was with William Houston's militia company along with Aaron Longstreet and possibly Silus Watters on January 20, 1777, at the notable Forage War battle near Abraham Van Nest's mill along the Millstone, two miles from Somerset Courthouse. Private Joseph Clark in Houston's company wrote that they were camped at Readington in Hunterdon County, when they met an express rider from General Washington ordering them immediately to Bound Brook under the command of General Philemon Dickinson.[74] At a bridge over the Millstone, Houston's men along with four hundred militia and fifty Pennsylvania Riflemen took on about five hundred British and Hessian foragers. The militia retreated twice but formed a third time. Amidst cannon fire from both sides, the British pouring grape shot into the Americans, the militia waded the icy river up to their waists and routed the enemy, capturing 43 baggage wagons, 104 horses, 115 head of cattle, and about 60 or 70 sheep. British officers were so surprised by the Americans' success that they swore with absolute certainty that "they were not militia, they were sure no militia would fight that way." Such *petite guerre* victories put the Jersey militia in high spirits and raised Washington's appreciation of the value of a well-led militia.[75]

In the weeks after the Battle of Princeton, James Moore as acting captain of the Princeton Militia also took charge of prisoners

---

74. Joseph Clark (1751-1813), born in Elizabeth, New Jersey, was a student of William Houston at the college in 1777. He graduated in 1781, afterward studied theology and was ordained as pastor of the Allentown Presbyterian Church and later the Presbyterian Church at New Brunswick.

75. Glenn, *Houston*, 26-28; George Washington to John Hancock, January 22, 1777, in W.W. Abbott, ed., et al, *The Papers of George Washington, Revolutionary War Series* (Charlottesville, 1988), Vol. 8, 125; *Pennsylvania Journal* (Philadelphia), January 29, 1777.

in Nassau Hall and guarded ammunition and stores. In April, his company elected him captain. Aaron Longstreet had resigned as captain to assist his family who were grieving the deaths of their four young soldiers of Aaron's generation. Longstreet accepted appointment as Commissioner of Stores, which allowed him to remain close to home. James Stockton was elected first lieutenant, and James Hamilton ensign.[76] After patrolling the lines at Middlebrook and along the Millstone in the summer of 1777, Moore was appointed Commissary of Prisoners at Princeton by "fighting parson" James Caldwell of Elizabethtown and by recommendation of Governor Livingston. He was assigned "to take charge of any prisoners sent there and to accompany them wherever ordered."[77]

In late September, Moore received orders to join Washington's army in Pennsylvania. He and his men fought in the Battle of Germantown October 4, 1777. Two outer columns of militia flanked two inner columns of Continentals and boldly advanced on the full British army.[78] Hampered by delays and dense fog, the Americans were eventually driven back, but their courage and tenacity at Germantown convinced the French that they would be worthy allies.

During the week before Christmas in 1777, James Moore and his company were directly commanded by Governor Livingston.

---

76. "Election of Officers of Princetown Company, April 28, 1777," New Jersey State Archives.

77. Pension File W1060.

78. Pension File W1060.

Figure 37. The Benjamin Chew mansion, "Cliveden,"
that saw continuous action in the Battle of Germantown.
Painting by Edward Lamson Henry, 1874.

They served as his personal bodyguard while he presided over the Legislature that was meeting at Princeton.[79]

In June 1778, Washington's troops pursued the British army moving from Philadelphia across New Jersey to New York. After camping at Hopewell, American forces marched east to harass the British. General Charles Scott led one of the four columns of Washington's army, 1500 light infantry, past the doorstep of Silus Watters' home on the Pennington-Rocky Hill Road.[80] They were on their way to the Battle of Monmouth, the last great

---

79. "Payroll of Moore's Company of VanDike's Battalion commanded by Gov. Livingston, December 18-24, 1777," New Jersey State Archives.

80. "Map of the Continental Army Routes to Monmouth, June 1778," in Mark Edward Lender and Garry Wheeler Stone, *Fatal Sunday: George Washington, the*

battle in the North and the longest fought engagement of the war. Moore recalled: "On the morning of June 27th, '78, General Washington marched with his army both regular and militia except his [Moore's] company to Monmouth Court House. He was ordered by General Washington to remain with his company in Princeton as a guard for our magazines, stores, etc., and to receive all prisoners that might be sent here and placed under his charge and by him conducted to Philadelphia."[81] On July 1, the Council of Safety ordered Moore to submit a list of the names and regiments of all prisoners from the battle and provide twenty men with an officer to take the prisoners to Philadelphia. The large number of guards indicates many prisoners.[82] Moore's payroll record states that he took prisoners to both Philadelphia and Morristown. His fellow church members Stephen Morford and Lemuel Scudder assisted him in transporting them.[83]

During the rest of 1778, Moore guarded the lines between New York and New Jersey and protected the transport of clothes for the army from Princeton to Elizabethtown. Silus Watters and his brother-in-law Daniel Leigh served then under Moore as guards.[84] In 1779, Moore's company continued to patrol the lines "to prevent plundering and excursions of the enemy." In February,

Monmouth Campaign, and the Politics of Battle (University of Oklahoma Press, 2016), 160.

81. Pension Record W1060.

82. *Minutes of the Council of Safety of the State of New Jersey* (Jersey City: J.H. Lyon, 1872), 266.

83. "Payroll of Captain James Moore's Company, Second Battalion of Col. Van Dyke, June 19-July 3, 1778," New Jersey State Archives.

84. "Pay Roll of Capt. James Moore's Co. of Col. Van Dyke's Bertallion, Second of Summerset, October 7, 1778," New Jersey State Archives.

Moore ordered Sergeant Isaac Cool to conduct eight prisoners from Princeton to Elizabeth Town and deliver them to Elias Boudinot, Commissary of Prisoners for New Jersey. Boudinot in turn ordered Moore to escort several captured British sailors from Elizabeth Town to Princeton. He planned to exchange the sailors for American prisoners held on prison ships in New York.[85] Between patrols, Moore and his friends, including Samuel Stout, Jr., were employed by Quartermaster Robert Stockton carting provisions to the militia and Continental Army.[86]

The first week in June 1780, James Moore's company, including his neighbors Stephen Morford and Samuel Stout, Jr., and Silus Watters with Silus's brothers-in-law William Savidge, Jr., and Daniel Leigh, were ordered to Springfield, but they were relieved on June 15, in the words of Moore, "a few days before the skirmish."[87] June 23 in Springfield was a full battle and a critical victory for the Americans. If they had not held the Hobart Gap west of the town, the British would have attacked Washington at Morristown, and the war would have been over. In their stint before the battle, Moore and his men took orders from Baron Von Steuben in his first field command of Continental troops and militia.[88] After Springfield, the war moved south.

On New Year's Day 1781, the Pennsylvania Line at Jockey Hollow, Morristown, mutinied demanding back pay, decent

---

85. Pension File W1060.

86. Certificates issued at Princeton by Robert Stockton, Q.M., January 15, 1780 and January 23, 1780. In Dorothy Agans Stratford, *Certificates and Receipts of Revolutionary New Jersey* (Lambertville: Hunterdon House), Vol. II, 204.

87. Pension File W1060.

88. See Thomas Fleming, *Forgotten Victory: The Battle for New Jersey, 1780* (New York: Readers Digest Press, 1973).

clothes and provisions, and overdue discharges. Fifteen hundred soldiers, closely tracked by General Anthony Wayne, set out over icy roads to present their demands to Congress in Philadelphia. But long malnourished and poorly clothed for winter, on January 3, they instead stopped and set up an orderly camp at Princeton. They chose a "Board of Sergeants," one man from each regiment to represent them. At the first news of the mutiny, Moore had been ordered to guard the state magazine at Princeton and all arms between Princeton and New Brunswick. Area militias mustered to protect local citizens and to counter any potential British aid to the mutineers. Two privates from the Hopewell company of Silus Watters' cousin Captain Philip Phillips billeted at Moore's house in case there was trouble.[89] Sympathetic to the Pennsylvania troops, however, Moore provided three horses to be used by them for four days.[90]

Joseph Reed, then president of the Pennsylvania Executive Council, arrived at Princeton on January 7 to confer with Wayne, the two to hear the demands. The mutineers were ready to negotiate. The Board of Sergeants proposed to honor Wayne and Reed with a cannon salute, but they were dissuaded that it would alarm the locals. Moore, in charge of arms at Princeton, probably advised the Board of Sergeants to abandon the noisy welcome.[91]

---

89. Pension File S1024.

90. Quartermaster Certificates, 166. James Moore per Gershom Moore, February 16, 1782 "for the service of three horse employed by the troops of the Pennsylvania Line four days in January 1781," New Jersey State Archives.

91. Pension File W1060; Pay Roll of James Moore of the Second Battalion "as a guard for guarding the State Magazine when the Pennsylvania Line revolted, January 6-14, 1780," New Jersey State Archives;" Michael Schellhammer,

Until the peace of 1783, James Moore "took care of prisoners, stores, and magazines," and led "excursions to prevent predatory parties of the enemy from New York and Staten Island."[92] He took a break from patrolling to celebrate Cornwallis's defeat at Yorktown. When news of the surrender reached Princeton in late October 1781, Beekman's Tavern hosted a dinner for the gentlemen of the town and neighborhood. The guests "enjoyed the occasion awhile with some good punch and wine." Then Moore's militia formed on the green in front of the tavern and fired off thirteen rounds from their cannon followed by an address by a college professor, quite likely William Houston. A public dinner followed at which thirteen toasts were drunk. The party broke up at six in the evening, and as darkness descended the village was illuminated and the militia again fired thirteen rounds.[93]

From the time of his courageous charge at Nassau Hall to his vigilant defense of farms and towns from marauding British during the Forage Wars, James Moore earned wide respect from New Jersey's revolutionary leaders. Celebrating the peace treaty with select distinguished patriots, Governor Livingston invited his sometime bodyguard and his wife, Phebe, to a formal dance at Mr. Cape's French Arms Tavern in Trenton on Wednesday, April 16, 1783.[94] In proper dress for the occasion, Moore would have

---

"Mutiny of the Pennsylvania Line," *Journal of the American Revolution*, January 14, 2014, https://allthingsliberty.com/2014/mutiny-pennsylvania-line/.

92. Pension File W1060.

93. *New Jersey Gazette*, October 31, 1781.

94. Hageman, *Princeton*, I, 190. John Cape was proprietor of the French Arms, a tavern in Trenton that had a twenty- by forty-three-foot space called "the long room," a popular venue for dances. The Continental Congress met there in 1784. www.history.state.gov/departmenthistory/buildings/section10.

worn his dog-head sword. He certainly would have worn it at the unforgettable September 1783 commencement of the college held in the partially restored Presbyterian Church. On the platform with Witherspoon sat the entire Congress, which was meeting in Princeton, the Ministers of France and Holland, General Washington, and young Ashbel Green, the valedictorian of the day. In his address, Green lauded Washington as "the man whose prudent conduct and whose gallant sword taught the tyrants of the earth to fear oppression and opened an asylum for the virtuous and free to all the world." Washington blushed.[95]

James Moore wore many hats for half a century after the war. He served on the Town Committee throughout the 1790s. For three decades he kept the roads in repair as one of several road overseers. Once he was Surveyor of Highways. In road meetings he assessed local travel conditions with Silus Watters, who oversaw the road from the Province Line to Rocky Hill (now Cherry Valley Road).[96]

In 1790, James Moore and Robert Stockton founded the Princeton Academy. Constructed on the church's lot in town, it was a school for younger students. Its charter proposed: "an institution for the instruction . . . in the various branches of literature, and for the encouragement and security of the generous and liberal minded." Subscribers paid Moore and Stockton and thereby

---

95. Hageman, *Princeton,* I, 170; Varnum Lansing Collins, *President Witherspoon* (New York: Arno Press, 1969), 133-134; Ashbel Green, *The Life of Ashbel Green* (New York: R. Carter and Bros., 1849), 143-144.

96. Town Book of the Western Precinct of Somerset, 1770-1860, Hopewell Museum.

became "proprietors and directors."[97] Steadfastly devoted to the Presbyterian Church, Moore contributed to its repair in 1784, served as trustee from 1786 to 1831, and as ruling elder from 1807 until his death in 1832.[98]

James Moore surely attended the celebrated visit of Lafayette to Princeton in September 1824 during the hero's farewell tour of America. Ladies and gentlemen of the town were presented to Lafayette where he was "publically received on a covered platform in front of the college and welcomed in an address by Richard Stockton, Jr. The concourse of people anxious to see the noble Marquis . . . was very large and enthusiastic."[99]

In his last years, Moore was blind and led about the town by a boy. With his other senses heightened by his loss of sight, he claimed to be weather-wise, and those who met him on his daily walks questioned him as an oracle of the weather.[100] In his will, he left assets to his wife, Abigail, including "all my plate," and to his niece Margaret Montgomery. But in a codicil, he removed Margaret and added his nieces Sarah Vandergrift of Trenton and Ann Allen of Philadelphia. He bequeathed the bulk of his estate to the trustees of the Presbyterian Church at Princeton. James Moore died November 29, 1832.

Although in the community he "commanded great respect for his patriotism and courage and for his military character and

---

97. Hageman, *Princeton*, I, 218-219. Subscribers included Enos Kelsey, Joseph Leigh, Aaron Mattison, Samuel Stout, Jr., Richard Longstreet, William Scudder, Abraham Cruser, Richard Stockton, Jr., Stephen Morford, Robert Stockton, James Moore.

98. Hageman, *Princeton*, I, 190.

99. Hageman, *Princeton*, I, 237-238.

100. Hageman, *Princeton*, I, 189-190.

services," his next of kin seemed less appreciative of his record. In his pension application three months before his death, Moore lamented that his family recently destroyed his Revolutionary War captain's commission certificate from Governor Livingston and most of his other papers, "supposing they would be of no further use."[101]

His inventory, taken in February 1833, included no sword, but listed many mahogany tables and chairs, desks, bookcases, carpets, looking glasses, and an eight-day clock, showing that he lived comfortably and well above average.[102] Abigail survived James fifteen years and died March 21, 1847.

---

101. Hageman, *Princeton,* I, 189-190; Pension File W1060.

102. Somerset County Will and Inventory, No. 2443R.

CHAPTER 6

Silus Watters in the War

Silus Watters

O n September 25, 1778, Silus Watters and his friend Daniel Manning enlisted together for a stint in James Moore's
militia. Discharged on October 7, they hastened back to the house
where Silus lived, the home of Silus's father- and mother-in-law,
William and Elizabeth Savidge, northwest of the village on the
south side of the Pennington-Rocky Hill Road at the Province
Line.[1] Daniel operated a distillery there at a spring next to the

---

1. The road from Pennington to Rocky Hill was officially declared a "great
road" about 1740, its upkeep the responsibility of the communities through which
it passed. Ursula C. Brecknell, *Montgomery Township: An Historic Community
1702-1972* (Montgomery Township Bicentennial Committee, 1972), 76. In the
1784 tax assessment, "Silass Waters" was listed as a "householder," showing that
he did not own the house in which he lived, with eight members in the household,
presumably Silus, his wife and children, and his wife's parents, who owned the
house. Tax Assessment List, Western Precinct, Somerset County, 1784, 12. New
Jersey State Archives.

OCTOBER

Figure 38. Cider pressing at a New Jersey farm. An engraving from Peter Watters' copy of *Farmer's Almanac for 1883*, printed by Matthias Plum, Newark, New Jersey. Plum used engravings from the almanac of his predecessor, Benjamin Olds, 1808.

Savidges' house. The still ran constantly in late fall when local farmers brought their home-pressed cider to be distilled into potent applejack known as "Jersey Lightning." Three weeks before he and Silus enlisted, Manning placed notice in the newspaper that he "continues to carry on the distillery at William Savidge's within four miles of Princeton, where he intends . . . to give satisfaction to all who please to favor him with their custom . . . as he has already provided a number of hogsheads in order to relieve those that are sent with the commodities that are to be distilled, and as casks at present become a scarce article. N.B. Said Manning proposes to distill at the moderate rate of one gallon of the spirit each barrel will produce when distilled."[2]

By the end of the war, Silus was serving the applejack at the tavern he kept in the Savidge house next to the still. He likely took charge of the distillery in 1781, when Manning left the business to

---

2. *New Jersey Gazette*, September 2, 1778, 3.

set up a brewery instead.[3] Two of Silus's relatives were noted tavern keepers. His cousin Philip Phillips, his captain in the militia and one of Washington's night guides to Trenton, kept a tavern in the center of Maidenhead.[4] In a stone house where the road from Princeton to Trenton crossed Eight Mile Run, Silus's maternal aunt Ruth Titus Phillips (1738-1818) and uncle William Phillips (1736-1778) managed the oldest "house of entertainment" in Maidenhead. When William died, Aunt Ruth continued to carry on the business. Silus learned from her.[5]

In contrast to James Moore's family who destroyed his papers, the Watters kept traditions. On May 15, 1751, in Hopewell, Priscilla Titus Watters (ca.1720-1806) named her second son Silas after her grandfather Silas Titus (1677-1748) of Newtown, Long Island. Her son Silas always signed his name "Silus," perhaps hearkening far back to the spelling of his great-great-great-great-grandfather of London, Silus Titus (1571-1637). In 1820, Silus Watters' son John (1787-1877) of Lebanon Township named his first son Ephraim Titus Watters after John's great-grandfather Ephraim Titus (1696-1789), who was a revered elder of the Pennington Presbyterian Church. These long-remembered names evidenced pride in family history and storytelling about worthy forebears. The Watters held to what

---

3. *New Jersey Gazette*, August 1, 1781, 4. Daniel Manning (1745-1835) was son of Ephraim Manning and Elizabeth Fitzrandolph (1708-1785) of Stoney Brook. www.geni.com/people/DanielManning6000000001869956844.

4. "A Map of the Road from Trenton to Amboy," in *New Jersey Road Maps of the Eighteenth Century* (Princeton University Library, 1964).

5. Cooley, *Genealogy*, 188; Charles Boyer, *Old Inns and Taverns in West Jersey* (Camden: Camden County Historical Society, 1962), 208.

Figure 39. A house divided. Detail of map of the court-ordered division of lands of William Savidge, Sr., 1821. One property line is "through the dwelling house by the middle of the wall." Note to the left of the house is a "spring of water" that supplied a still.

Abraham Lincoln would call "the mystic chords of memory that stretch back to patriots' graves."[6]

While the Watters were proud of their past, their estate debacles eventually clouded memories of it. They failed to leave wills, even though Silus and his son John were justices of the peace. When Silus's father-in-law, William Savidge, Sr., died in Princeton in 1807, Silus and his brother, Foster, contested a "pretended" will. In the dispute they retained Richard Stockton, Jr., as counsel. At the time of Silus's death fourteen years later, the estate still was not settled. Three court-appointed commissioners finally divided the real estate among heirs, including Silus's widow, Sarah

6. Lincoln was quoted by Michael Beschloss, Interview with Judy Woodruff, Public Broadcasting System, February 6, 2020. For Titus genealogy see www .Geni.com/people/11ᵗʰ-Robert-Titus/6000000000426688430.

Savidge Watters. The Savidge farm of 225 acres was carved into thirteen small parcels. One dividing line ran straight "through the dwelling house by the middle of the wall," giving half the house to William and Elizabeth's daughter Elizabeth Savidge and the other half to her sister Ann Savidge Lyon.[7] One hopes they got along. Silus himself seemed to have learned no lesson from his troubles, and he died intestate at sixty-nine in 1820. His son John also died without a will at ninety in 1877. Both left large estates, the division of which launched lawsuits and bitter grudges.

Silus was only sixteen when his father, Thomas, died in Maidenhead in 1767 at age forty-four. Silus's earlier forebears lived longer. His maternal grandfather, Ephraim Titus, the elder in the Pennington Presbyterian Church, lived to ninety-three. His great-great-grandfather Anthony Waters [sic], an attorney born in Plymouth, Massachusetts, as a widower married at age ninety-two and lived to one hundred. [8]

Thomas Watters left his widow, Priscilla, with eight children to raise, all under the age of twenty-one. A decade earlier, when Joseph Moore died, he also left his wife, Helena, with eight children, several, including James, under legal age.[9] Alike in their losses, and part of the same Pennington Church flock, the Moores

7. Receipt of Silus Watters, administrator of William Savidge, Sr., Watters Papers; Real Estate of William Savidge, late of Montgomery Township, August 1821, Somerset County Surrogate, Estate Book A, 166ff, map follows 175. No record of the court case is extant. The division of the house may indicate that the William and Elizabeth Savidge dwelling had been physically divided since the time when Silus and Sarah Savidge Watters lived with William and Elizabeth and kept a tavern in their half of the house.

8. "Descendants of Andrew Waters," www.smithsworldwide.org/tng/media /gen_rpt_waters.pdf.

9. Hunterdon County Will No. 411.

gave moral support to the Watters in their time of sorrow. James earlier knew the same grief that now weighed on his friend Silus.

Less advantaged than the Moores, Silus and his siblings had to make it on their own. By the beginning of the war, Silus was married to Sarah Savidge, and they were living with her parents. His brother, Foster, two years older, was married to Sarah's sister Rachel, and either living with the Savidges or nearby. Both Silus and Foster resided in the Western Precinct, "near Princeton," according to Foster's Revolutionary War pension application. In 1777, Foster moved into Hopewell to a modest twenty acres on the Province Line close to the Savidge farm, and he owned one horse and one cow.[10]

Silus was twenty-five when in December 1776 the British occupied Princeton. From then until the Continental Congress left in 1783, Princeton either in action or authority was, in the words of James Moore, "the seat of war." Silus and his family lived in the thick of the turmoil for seven years. He knew the horror and heroism of the conflict that besieged his extended family and neighbors. When the dog-head sword became his, most likely after the war, Silus's wartime experiences and those in the stories told by friends at his tavern became one with the sword, emblem of Moore's bravery at Nassau Hall and symbol of all the memories of the Revolution.

Princeton was a center of political activism for a decade before the war. The leadership of Silus's pastor, John Witherspoon, champion of American rights, reached beyond the college and the church to all the colonies. On a Congressional Day of Fasting,

---

10. 1780 Tax List; Pension File 11100. An 1812 deed references Francis Vannoy as the previous owner of Foster Watters' property in Hopewell.

May 17, 1776, Witherspoon preached his most famous and widely published sermon, "The Dominion of Providence over the Passions of Men." In it he argued that independence was the only logical course of action open to Americans and that Providence was on the side of the colonies.[11]

Silus was probably in the crowd with James Moore that gathered in front of Nassau Hall on the night of July 9, 1776, to hear the Declaration of Independence read, when the college was "grandly illuminated" and "independency proclaimed under a triple volley of musketry."[12] But five months later the college was deserted, and almost all local people fled as British troops advanced on the town. The Stocktons evacuated with their slaves to Freehold, the Witherspoons rode a horse and gig to Pennsylvania, and John Hart of Hopewell, signer of the Declaration, had to leave his dying wife and hide out in the Sourland Mountains. Lydia Spencer, the daughter of Trenton minister Elihu Spencer, remarked that the crowd at the Trenton ferry "called up the day of judgment, so many frightened people were assembled . . . all flying for their lives."[13]

No place near Princeton escaped destruction by the British and Hessians. Livestock was slaughtered or driven off, crops, orchards, and fences destroyed, houses stripped of everything. British soldiers billeted in all the houses and outbuildings.[14] Silus's

---

11. John Witherspoon, *The Dominion of Providence over the Passions of Men*, (Philadelphia: R. Aitken, 1776).

12. *Pennsylvania Packet*, July 15, 1776.

13. Ralph Ege, *Pioneers of Old Hopewell with Sketches of Her Revolutionary Heroes* (Race and Savidge, 1908), 29-30; Barber and Howe, *Historical Collections*, 262.

14. Ege, *Pioneers,* 31.

home on a main road only three miles from town must have been occupied or ransacked by soldiers. When Washington retreated into Pennsylvania, Silus's brother Foster, who lived with him or nearby, "went into Kingwood," to avoid the British, "where he had the smallpox and was detained there with it 'til after the Battle of Princeton." [15] What Silus and his immediate family endured— and whether they fled or stayed—is unknown, but the suffering of his relatives and damage to places he loved spun stories that are recounted to this day.

Rick Atkinson would write, "The King's men pillaged with a methodical vengeance."[16] An account published on December 12, 1776, reported, "Maidenhead and Hopewell are entirely broken up. The houses are stripped of every article of furniture, and what is not portable is entirely destroyed." [17] General Nathaniel Greene wrote the governor of Rhode Island that the "ravages in the Jerseys exceeds all description. Men slaughtered, women ravished, and houses plundered. Little girls not ten years old ravished. Mothers and daughters ravished in the presence of their husbands and sons."[18]

---

15. Pension File 11100.

16. Atkinson, *The British Are Coming*, 457.

17. Alfred Hoyt Bill, *New Jersey and the Revolutionary War* (New Brunswick: Rutgers University Press, 1964), 24; "Conduct of the British and Hessian Troops in New Jersey, December 12, 1776," in Peter Force, *American Archives, Fifth Series: A Documentary History of the United States of America* (Washington, D.C., 1853), III, 1188.

18. "Extract of a letter from an officer of distinction in the American Army," *Pennsylvania Packet*, December 27, 1776, 1.

Reuben Armitage was Silus Watters' great-uncle, brother of Silus's maternal grandmother, Mary Armitage Titus. Reuben lived just two miles southwest of Silus on the same road. He had inherited the farm of his father, Enoch Armitage, which lay west of the bridge over the Stoney Brook in Hopewell.[19] Reuben was old and blind, and when the British entered Princeton, his hired hands and slaves all fled except one slave named Cato. A British foraging party found Cato and Reuben in the house and "abused them in most brutal manner." The regulars broke glass, china, looking glasses, and earthenware, and smashed all the furniture and burned it. They ripped open the feather ticks to use as sacks for their plunder. Outside they killed the poultry and pigs and rounded up the cattle to drive back to camp in Princeton. Then they beat Reuben and threatened to kill him if he did not tell them where he had hidden his money and valuables. He did not tell, but they found freshly dug soil and discovered his buried treasure. They drove Reuben into the woods and left him to die in the freezing weather, but his daughters found him and saved his life.[20] We do not know what happened to Cato.

As well as physical assaults on his family, Silus saw the desecration of the churches that formed and sustained him. The British used both the Princeton and Pennington churches for barracks. In Princeton they chopped up the pews on the main floor and in the gallery for firewood, which they burned in an improvised stove. The situation at Pennington, where his mother,

---

19. Cooley, *Genealogy*, 270.

20. Letter of Benjamin Armitage, February 21, 1843, to Cyrus Armitage in Cyrus Armitage, *Some Account*, 61-62.

Priscilla, and grandfather Ephraim still worshipped, was the same or worse. From December 9-14, 1776, Lord Cornwallis bivouacked at Pennington with over a thousand men. After five days, the village was in shambles. A hundred soldiers billeted in the meeting house and similarly hacked the pews which they burned inside in makeshift brick stoves. They brought their horses in to make it warmer. The marble top altar table, the gift from James Moore's cousin Moore Furman, and from which the families of Silus and James received communion, was smashed by a blow from a British gun. The troops exercised their horses by jumping them over the churchyard walls into the burial ground, profaning the consecrated space and injuring the graves of generations of Silus's family. Adding insult, on December 13, 1776, the brash young British lieutenant Banastre Tarleton and his thirty light horsemen arrived with their prized new captive, General Charles Lee. They celebrated and partied into the night, toasting the King and getting Lee's horse drunk.[21]

Silus's extended family were leaders in the conflict. His Phillips relatives furnished several officers, including Captain Jonathan Phillips, an original member of the Society of the Cincinnati, and more than a dozen soldiers for the American side. Philip Phillips was Silus's sometime captain in the militia. Thomas Phillips served with Silus's brother, Foster, in Captain Israel Carle's Trenton light horse troop. Silus personally knew many of the eighteen local men who guided Washington's army along stormy night

---

21. York, *Pennington Presbyterians*, 80, 83; Atkinson, *The British Are Coming*, 504; http://williamgreenhouse.org/green_family/gen/lydia.html.

roads to the Battle of Trenton. Half of them were his cousins.[22] Gideon Lyon (1742-1814), Silus's brother-in-law married to Ann Savidge (1755-1817), fought at the Battle of Long Island in August 1776 and in skirmishes on Manhattan in the days following.[23]

Silus's Aunt Ruth and Uncle William Phillips could recite the details of the bloody standoff that erupted near their tavern on the east side of Eight Mile Run near Maidenhead on New Year's Day 1777. Washington had ordered a thousand men and several cannons to delay Cornwallis's expected march from Princeton to Trenton. Under heavy fire, the Americans held the high west banks of the creek at "the pass" where the road ran between hills. The fight lasted all morning until the British brought up their own cannons and drove them back. One hundred forty men, mostly British, perished there in the din of battle.[24]

Only three of Silus Watters' payroll records from the war survive, but he probably served along with his brother, Foster, at least early in the war, since they both were in their mid-twenties and lived in the same place. Foster served early in 1776 under Captain William Churchill Houston, professor at the college, and in New York City "when the British fleet hove into sight at the Hook." After sequestering in Kingwood with smallpox during the Battle of Princeton, Foster Watters took up residence in Hopewell and

---

22. Cousins: Philip Phillips, Elias Phillips, John Phillips, Joseph Phillips, John Muirhead, Ephraim Woolsey, Edon Burroughs, Stephen Burroughs, Amos Scudder. See Larry Kidder, "Guiding Washington to Trenton," *Journal of the American Revolution*, May 6, 2014.

23. Ege, *Pioneers*, 266.

24. Joseph P. Tustin, ed., *Johann Ewald, Diary of the American War: A Hessian Journal* (New Haven: Yale University Press, 1979), 48; Fischer, *Washington's Crossing*, 281, 525 notes 14, 17.

served in the Hunterdon militia under Captain Ralph Guild and Colonel Joab Houghton in General Heard's brigade. He was at the Battle of Monmouth under Captain Guild, Colonel Houghton, and Colonel Joseph Phillips "where the bullets flew like hail." "General Lee was in front of the militia and was to lead on the battle, but he retreated and met General Washington who ordered his sword to be taken from him. We should have had a nice little fight, if Lee had stood." After Monmouth, Foster joined the light horse troop of Captain Carle of Trenton and continued with Carle "until after the peace was made."[25]

James Moore also served in Captain Houston's company in 1776 before becoming lieutenant in that company in August, when Aaron Longstreet replaced Houston as captain. James and Foster and probably Silus served first and early together as privates.[26]

During the week before the Battle of Princeton of January 3, 1777, private Joseph Clark of Captain Houston's makeshift militia company reported that the British took some men of his company prisoners near Princeton.[27] Robert Lawrence, eyewitness of the Battle of Princeton, remembered that when the British surrendered and strode out of Nassau Hall, they were followed by American prisoners—Continentals and thirty local "country people that were accused either of being rebels or aiding and assisting them."[28] If perchance Silus were one of the prisoners liberated from Nassau Hall by his sword-wielding friend, James Moore, or

---

25. Pension File 11100.

26. Glen, *Houston*, 19-20. The records of Houston's company no longer exist.

27. Glen, *Houston*, 24.

28. Lawrence, *A Brief Narrative*, 34.

if Silus were one of the men who helped him storm the door, what a memento that dog-head sword would have been for him.

The first extant record of Silus in the war shows him enrolled for three weeks, September 14, 1777, to October 7, 1777, as corporal in the company of his cousin Captain Philip Phillips of the First Regiment of the Hunterdon County Militia. Phillips was one of Washington's guides to Trenton, and he kept a tavern in Maidenhead.[29] The British occupied Philadelphia on September 26, 1777, and the State Legislature meeting at Princeton was apprehensive for its own safety. Governor Livingston ordered part of Phillips' company to be "on command at Princeton."

As corporal, Silus Watters took orders from his immediate superior, Second Lieutenant Elias Hunt (1746-1820). Watters and his cohorts knew the story of Hunt's recent narrow escape from a Hessian Jaeger. On the morning of the Second Battle of Trenton, January 2, 1777, as an advance guard of mounted Jaegers entered Maidenhead from Princeton, they spied Hunt on horseback on the road ahead. They took out after him at a gallop. One of them caught up to Hunt and raised his sword about to cut him down. In the nick of time, a hidden American picket near the Maidenhead church shot and wounded the Hessian, but he continued in pursuit. Then there were two more shots heard, and both the Jaeger and his horse fell dead. The Jaeger was buried on the farm of Silus's cousin Colonel Joseph Phillips in Hopewell.[30]

Exactly a year later, from September 25, 1778, to October 7, 1778, Silus Watters served as a private in James Moore's company

---

29. Muster Roll No. 689, New Jersey State Archives.

30. Extract of a letter from a respectable inhabitant, dated Lawrenceville, August 22, 1816, in Wilkinson, *Memoirs*. Vol. 1, 136.

in Colonel Henry Van Dyke's Second Somerset Battalion. It was an opportune time of the year for farmers to perform militia duty after crops were harvested and fodder pulled. The company continued to patrol for British foragers and to transport supplies between army depots. Joining Watters were his brother-in-law Daniel Leigh, his friend Daniel Manning who managed the still on the Savidge farm, and William Hyer from the family of Jacob Hyer, Sr., innkeeper of the popular Hudibras Tavern in Princeton, a storied place of revolutionary gatherings.[31]

Watters again joined Moore's company in Colonel Van Dyke's battalion for the week of June 8-15, 1780, at Springfield. They took orders in the field from Baron Von Steuben. At the end of that week, Moore remembered, the unit "was relieved a few days before the skirmish." Watters enrolled along with two brothers-in-law, William Savidge, Jr., and Daniel Leigh, and his friend Samuel Stout, Jr., the silversmith in Princeton.[32] The farm of Samuel Stout's parents where he was raised was a short walk west over the Province Line in Hopewell from where Watters lived.

31. Jacob Hyer's son William, born 1766, if his birth year is correct, would barely have been a teenager in 1778, too young to be a sergeant, as listed. Jacob Hyer also had cousins in Somerset County named William, so this William may have been one of them. Both Jacob's older son, Jacob, Jr., born 1763, and his son, William, became members of the Society of the Cincinnati. *The Institution of the Society of the Cincinnati in the State of New Jersey* (Albany: J. Munsell, 1866), 39; "Payroll of Capt. James Moore's Company of Milichia of Cornel Vandikes Bertallon, Second of Somerset, October 7, 1778," New Jersey State Archives.

32. "Payroll of Capt. James Moore's Company, Col. Van Dike's Battalion, at Springfield, June 8-15, 1780," New Jersey State Archives; Pension File W1060.

Figure 40. Haying at a New Jersey farm. An engraving from Peter Watters' copy of *Farmer's Almanac for 1883*, after Benjamin Olds, 1808.

The payroll roster of Moore's Springfield deployment shows that sometime during the week Silus Watters, his brother-in-law William Savidge, Jr., and his neighbor Samuel Stout, Jr., deserted—probably together. Most desertions, which were fairly common in the militia, occurred according to necessities of the farming year. June was the first haying month in central New Jersey. Neighbors at times of harvest—in this instance the Watters, Savidges, and Stouts—always depended on working together to bring in their crops, sharing their labor as part of the exchange farming economy.

Although the militia was criticized for desertions, being called out for duty not only made feeding one's family difficult, but also reduced food available for men and horses in the army. "Deserting" did not mean militia had abandoned the cause or were cowardly, only that they could not do two things at the same time. Many men who were fined for not turning out or even court-martialed for deserting later had their fines returned and court-martials lifted, when they explained their circumstances.[33] Haying was an artfully timed harvest tied to a variable window that depended on the condition of the grass and the necessity of clear weather. No record exists of any fine levied or court-martial imposed on Silus and his friends for their early exit nor any indication of lasting disfavor in the eyes of Captain Moore.

---

33. Email from Larry Kidder to J. Lawrence Brasher, January 9, 2020.

CHAPTER 7

"A Proper Person to Keep a Tavern"

They lived in interlinked networks of kindred, neighbors, and fellow members of churches and militia companies.
Daniel W. Patterson, *The True Image*

I would ask for the stories, the voice of memory over the land.
Barry Lopez, *American Geographies*

Silus Watters celebrated every Christmas by treating the patrons of his Province-Line tavern to a merry party, where, along with feasting, drinking, singing, and storytelling, neighbors could sign his tavern license application. Every innkeeper in New Jersey was required annually to petition the court with twelve approving signatures of county freeholders. This was the way the colony regulated the sale and distribution of alcohol.[1]

---

1. Boyer, *Old Inns*, 11.

Christmas in Princeton blended lively English, Dutch, and German customs with devout religious observances. Holiday feasts included ham, beef, goose, turkey, oysters, pies filled with fowl and game, puddings, plum cakes, and mince pies. Ben Franklin quipped, "Oh blessed season! Lov'd by Saints and Sinners, For long Devotions or for longer Dinners." Eighteenth-century pro-Christmas communities ate and drank their way through the Christmas holidays. Alcohol was always part of Christmas, a festival, a London magazine stated, "held sacred by good eating and drinking."[2] The men at Silus's parties could sing the verse of Yankee Doodle:

> Christmas is a-coming Boys,
> We'll go to Mother Chase's,
> And there we'll get a sugar dram
> Sweetened with Melasses.[3]

A typical rural New Jersey tavern consisted of at least two rooms, although Silus Watters' house with his in-laws must have been larger. One room contained the bar and tables for drinking and meals; the others served as residence quarters for the tavern keeper and family. The bar was usually in a corner of the dining room with a lockable door, a narrow ledge for ordering drinks, and a wooden barricade that swung down from the ceiling at night to close the bar known as a "cage bar."[4] In addition to the usual beer,

2. Boyer, *Old Inns*, 73; Penne L. Restad, *Christmas in America* (New York: Oxford University Press, 1995), 9.

3. Judith Flanders, *Christmas: A Biography* (New York: St. Martin's Press, 2017), 73.

4. Ben Ruset, "The Jersey Taverns," NJ Pine Barrens.com, September 2, 2011.

ale, cider, wine, and rum, taverns in eighteenth-century New Jersey served as many as forty different drinks. Most popular were:

Cyder Royall: Hard cider boiled to one-fourth its original volume.

Metheglin: A concoction of fermented honey, herbs, and water.

Mimbo: Rum and sugar.

Flip: A mixture of beer, rum, and sugar heated with a red-hot iron.[5]

Drinking was considered fashionable in eighteenth-century America. In day-to-day tavern life incidents of drunkenness were the exception, but some places and occasions were reliably rowdy.[6] James Moore's friend Captain Erkuries Beatty, wartime hero, frolicker, and later mayor of Princeton, in 1783 celebrated St. Patrick's Day in a Philadelphia tavern and described the assorted gathering in a letter to his brother: "A few reduced Continental officers, captains of ships, Irish volunteers, hatters' apprentices, sexton, bell-ringer, psalm singer . . . clerk of Christ Church, and doctor's mates on stages—damned droll sinners to be sure—in such mixed company did I spend the evening in a dirty, noisy tavern . . . where we held out 'til one o'clock and behaved exactly in character . . . A picked and select company it was too—I am now

---

5. Ruset, "Jersey Taverns;" In 1759, Israel Acrelius, a Swedish Lutheran minister in New Jersey, listed over forty alcoholic drinks popular in the colony. William Reynolds, ed., *Israel Acrelius, A History of New Sweden* (Stockholm, 1759), reprint, Philadelphia: Historical Society of Pennsylvania, 1876), 160-164.

6. Steven Strucinski, "The Tavern in Colonial America," *The Gettysburg Historical Journal*, Vol. 1 (2002), 38.

very thankful I am clear of it without my head being broke."[7] But most taverns toward the end of the eighteenth century tended to attract a "select," socially respectable clientele, where the middle and upper class "were happier drinking among their own kind," where, in the words of Princeton historian John Hageman, "distinguished soldiers, statesmen, divines, lawyers, scholars, and poets would meet and mingle for a few hours."[8] The Presbyterian Church in Princeton held congregational meetings in the town's taverns, and in the 1814 rebuilding of the church, superintended by James Moore, the carpenters were paid $1.50 and "three half gills of low-priced spirits" per day.[9] The widespread temperance movement did not take hold until later in the nineteenth century.

Taverns were public institutions, centers of social and political life. Along with alcohol, patrons in the barroom could play games, join in discussion, and hear the latest news. Farmers, storekeepers, and gentry debated the issues of the time. Taverns pulled fledgling communities together.[10] Tavern keepers had to be men and women of character in order to obtain a license, and their role required them to be social beings. Landlords, in the words of Hageman, "always had to be ready to tell a good story and sing a good song." [11]

---

7. Erkuries Beatty to Reading Beatty, March 20, 1783, in Joseph Beatty, "Letters of the Four Beatty Brothers," 234.

8. Peter Thompson, *Rum, Punch, and Revolution, Tavern Going and Public Life in Eighteenth-Century Philadelphia* (Philadelphia: University of Pennsylvania Press, 1999), 149; Hageman, *Princeton*, II, 36.

9. Hageman, *Princeton*, II, 38, 109.

10. Strucinski, *The Tavern*, 29.

11. Hageman, *Princeton*, II, 39.

Taverns in New Jersey proliferated immediately after the war. Returning veterans created a flood of tavern licenses. In 1786, Governor Livingston complained: "I have seen four times as many taverns in the state as are necessary. These superabundant taverns are continuously haunted by idlers."[12] After the war, preference in granting licenses was given to veterans, so by 1783, a majority of taverns were kept by colonels, captains, widows of soldiers, or any ex-service man.[13]

Conversation and gossip were the chief entertainment. And in the 1780s the stories were of the war. Longfellow wrote of the imagined patrons at the Wayside Inn: "Each had his tale to tell, and/ Was anxious to be pleased and please;" they recounted "Legends that once were told or sung/ In many a smoky fireside nook."[14]

The first extant tavern application of Silus Watters, in January 1788, attested that he was "a proper person to keep a tavern" and certified that he had "kept a house of entertainment for some time past at the house where he now lives," so one may assume

---

12. Theodore Sedgwick, *A Memoir of the Life of William Livingston* (New York: J & J. Harper, 1833), 394.

13. Boyer, *Old Inns*, 8.

14. "Tales of a Wayside Inn," in Henry Wadsworth Longfellow, *Complete Poetical Works* (Boston: Houghton, Mifflin, & Co., 1885), 181, 190; A description of Hopewell Colonel Joab Houghton's storytelling epitomizes conversations at Silus's tavern: "The old colonel was of a very jovial disposition and loved a good story, and after the close of the war [his] old house was a favorite place for the old veterans to gather, and seated before the wide fireplace they loved to talk over the exciting experiences of the camp, the march and the battlefield, and the 'burning memories of that glorious drama of freedom,' in which they bore such a noble part." Ege, *Pioneers*, 19.

that he was an innkeeper since close to the end of the war.[15] Silus's two parties of record were held on Christmas Eve 1787 and the day after Christmas 1789. A total of twenty-four neighbor guests signed the tavern applications. Three signers attended both parties. Relatives of Silus were probably also present but were not eligible to sign the license application. The celebrating freeholders signed in this order:

December 24, 1787

Thomas Stockton	Joseph Stryker
Garrett Van Pelt	Timothy Baker
Isaac Stryker	John Scott
John Roberson	Ichabod Leigh
Aaron Mattison	Enoch Elberson
Abraham Voorhees	Henry Berrien
Daniel Slack	Jerimiah Van Dike [sic]

December 26,1789

Daniel Slack	Joseph Leigh
Abraham Voorhees	T.W. Montgomery
Benjamin Hunt	Zebulon Stout
Henry Berrien	Nicholas Golden
Richard Sutphen	Varnell Hunt

Who were they? Where were they in the war, and what did they witness? What stories could they tell? Were some connected to James Moore? Just over three miles from Princeton village,

---

15. Somerset County, New Jersey, Tavern Applications, 1788, 1790, New Jersey State Archives.

116

Silus occasionally served residents of the town, but the lists show that most customers were his neighbors—farmers, artisans, and gentry from along the Province Line, from Bedens Brook, the Rocky Hill-Pennington Road, and Blawenburg. Many of them were related to each other by blood or marriage and to others of note in the Revolution.

Henry Berrien (1746-1806)

The Berriens were the leading local gentry, anchored in the person of Judge John Berrien (1711-1772), who was Henry Berrien's uncle.[16] In 1783, George Washington lived for three months at "Rockingham," the home of Judge Berrien's widow, Margaret, six miles east on Silus's road at Rocky Hill. Invited to Princeton while Congress was meeting there, Washington wrote his farewell address to the Army at Rockingham.

On April 22, 1772, John Berrien, who was a Justice of the New Jersey Supreme Court, trustee of the college at Princeton, and a member of the New Jersey Colonial Assembly, invited his friends, including Richard Stockton, to Rockingham to witness his will. After signing, he took them on a stroll down the hill to the Millstone River and threw himself into the chilly deep water and drowned.

In the late summer and fall of 1783, Washington rented the twenty-room Berrien country estate from Margaret Berrien. Washington's bodyguard of twenty or thirty soldiers camped

---

16. Specific genealogy sources (dates, lines of descent, marriages, etc.) will not be cited in this section on tavern patrons. They are too numerous to include and most are on line. When possible, multiple sources have been consulted, and the information is as accurate as could be determined.

Figure 41. Rockingham, Washington's
headquarters in Rocky Hill, 1783.

around the house, and George and Martha held dinners for as
many as two hundred distinguished guests from throughout the
states, including Thomas Jefferson, James Madison, and Thomas
Paine. The overflow crowds dined in a marquee on the lawn. At
Rockingham, Washington received word of the signing of the
Treaty of Paris on October 31, 1783.

The Washingtons enjoyed their well-deserved relaxed
social life at the "very healthy and finely situated farm" with
its orchards and expansive views of the Watchung Mountains
to the north and the Hopewell Valley to the west.[17] Washington took frequent horseback rides into the countryside and
often stopped to visit his friend John Van Horne (died 1820)
at his farm on Silus's road west of the Millstone River. A local

17. *Rivington's Royal Gazette*, July 5, 1783, advertisement for sale of
Rockingham.

character anecdote about Van Horne and General Washington must have been told at Silus's tavern, perhaps by Henry Berrien: Van Horne was uncommonly large and strong. A roast pig was on the menu for a dinner to which Washington was invited. One of Van Horne's slaves was trying in vain to catch the pig, so Van Horne threw off his coat and hat, caught the squealing pig, held it up in mud-spattered, sweaty triumph, and yelled to his slave, "I'll show ye how to run down a pig!" And as he shouted, he looked up into the face of Washington who had just trotted into the yard. It was, the story goes, one of the rare times that Washington shook with laughter.[18]

Henry Berrien purchased his farm of 195 acres from John Van Horne a few years before the pig incident.[19] His home stood somewhere between Van Horne's house and Silus's tavern. Henry's father was Peter Berrien (1714-1781), brother of Judge Berrien. As nephew of the Judge and Margaret, Henry probably attended some of Washington's gala dinners at Rockingham. Henry married Cornelia Van Dyke (1743-1824) in 1765.[20] This is where the family relationships begin to get dense. In eighteenth-century rural America, brothers and sisters in one family often married sisters and brothers from a neighboring farm family. Henry Berrien's sister Elizabeth Berrien (1740-1780) was married to Henry's

---

18. William Dunlap, *A History of the Rise and Progress of the Arts of Design in the United States* (Boston: C.E. Goodspeed and Company, 1918), 298-299.

19. All citations of acreage owned by the tavern patrons are from Fred Sisser, "Reconstructed 1790 Census of Somerset County," *Somerset County Genealogical Quarterly*, vo. 7, no. 2 (June 1990), 141-144.

20. The Van Dykes and the Berriens were Dutch and Huguenot families. They and their forebears were pillars of the Dutch Reformed Church at Six Mile Run northeast of Rocky Hill.

wife Cornelia's brother, Colonel Henry Van Dyke (1743-1817). Henry Van Dyke, twice brother-in-law of Henry Berrien, was Captain James Moore's immediate commanding officer in the Revolution for seven years from 1777 to the end of the war.[21] Moore and the Van Dykes and the Berriens were close associates.

Colonel Henry Van Dyke owned a mill on Bedens Brook about three miles northeast of Silus Watters and, like several other local Van Dykes, was wealthy. One of his orders for goods in the 1780s included "a pair of gloves for daughter" and "two china teapots."[22] As Town Clerk in December 1774, he was appointed to the Committee of Inspection for the Western Precinct charged with keeping their eyes on loyalists.[23] It was easy for Henry, since another of his sisters, Rebecca, was married to Lieutenant Colonel John Van Dyke, her cousin, who commanded the loyalist West Jersey Volunteers. In May 1779, Henry escorted Rebecca from Somerset County to meet her fugitive husband at Elizabethtown. Henry cross-examined his loyalist brother-in-law and provided Washington with the information that the British in New York were readying their boats for a military excursion up the Hudson.[24]

The year before, by order of the Princeton Committee of Safety, Henry Van Dyke with Moore's former captain, William

---

21. The same birth year is cited for Cornelia Van Dyke and her brother Henry. If correct, they were twins.

22. Brecknell, *Montgomery Township*, 216.

23. "Somerset Patriotism Preceding the Revolutionary War," *Somerset County Historical Quarterly,* vol. 5, no. 4 (October 1916), 241-242.

24. Edward G. Lengel, *The Papers of George Washington, Revolutionary War Series* (Charlottesville: University of Virginia Press, 2010), vol. 20, 588-589, Colonel Israel Shreve to George Washington, May 23, 1779.

Houston, had set up alarm beacons on Henry's farm to warn of British forays.[25] Henry commanded troops at the battles of Monmouth, Germantown, Connecticut Farms, and Springfield.[26] To celebrate the victory at Yorktown, Colonel Van Dyke attended a dinner and ball at George Morgan's "Prospect Farm" in Princeton along with the Berriens, General Heard, John Rutherfurd, and the Van Hornes.[27] Henry Van Dyke served as the first Town Clerk of the Western Precinct in 1772 and frequently for two decades after that. A member of the State Assembly in 1779, he was a Chosen Freeholder in 1787. He was on the town committee with James Moore 1793-1797.[28]

Adding pieces to the wide family quilt, a sister of Cornelia Van Dyke Berrien and Colonel Henry Van Dyke was Anne Van Dyke (1733-1810). Anne was the wife of Samuel Stout, Sr., (1731-1803) and mother of Samuel Stout, Jr. (1755-1796), the Princeton silversmith. Samuel, Jr., was a fellow private with Silus Watters and William Savidge, Jr., in James Moore's company at Springfield in June 1780, when the three of them deserted to cut hay.[29]

Henry Berrien was summoned in May 1778 along with twenty-three other freeholders to the home of Nicholas Golden, neighbor of Silus Watters east of the Great Road, to determine if

---

25. Hageman, *Princeton* I, 165.

26. Pension Record Private Hendrick Cortelyou, *Somerset County Historical Quarterly*, vol. 1, 231-232.

27. Don Skemer, "Revolutionary Times at Prospect Farm," *Princeton University Library Manuscript News,* August 11, 2016.

28. Snell, *Hunterdon and Somerset*, 842; Brecknell, *Montgomery Township*, 26.

29. Cornelia, Henry, Rebecca, and Anne Van Dyke were children of John and Charity Van Dyke of Bedens Brook.

Joseph Stockton, Princeton's most notorious accused loyalist, had joined the King's army and rejected allegiance to the State. The verdict was against Stockton, and his farm near the Princeton battlefield was forfeited and sold post-mortem. The unfortunate Joseph Stockton had died only a month after the battle. Also at the meeting were Joseph Stryker, at one of Silus's parties, and William Savidge, Sr., Silus's father-in-law.[30] Henry Berrien served as Tax Collector for the Western Precinct from 1789 to 1790.[31]

Thomas West Montgomery (1764-1820)

Thomas West Montgomery was married to Mary Berrien (1768-1850), daughter of Judge John Berrien and Margaret Berrien, so Mary was first cousin of Henry Berrien, above. Thomas Montgomery was a medical doctor admitted to practice in 1787 and at the time of Silus's 1789 party had recently returned from two years studying medicine in Paris. His Quaker grandfather, James Montgomery, emigrated as a child from Ayrshire, Scotland. Thomas's father, Alexander Montgomery (1735-1798) was a wealthy farmer of nearby Allentown, New Jersey. At the time of the party, Thomas Montgomery was practicing just a mile from Silus's tavern, west of the Province Line in Hopewell at Dogtown, later named Stoutsburg.[32] Afterward he practiced in the more

---

30. Hageman, *Princeton* I, 175.

31. Snell, *Hunterdon and Somerset*, 842.

32. David Blackwell email to J. Lawrence Brasher, March 22, 2018.

auspiciously named villages of Princeton and Allentown, and finally in New York City, where he is buried at Trinity Church.[33]

Proud of their Scottish heritage, both Thomas Montgomery and John Witherspoon were members of the Philadelphia Saint Andrew's Society that attended to the needs of Scottish immigrants. Witherspoon's country estate, Tusculum, lay about two miles from Silus Watters' tavern toward Princeton. It was probably Thomas Montgomery's father, Alexander, who stayed at and protected Tusculum from serious damage during the British occupation, while Witherspoon was a refugee in Pennsylvania. Alexander Montgomery was a trustee of the Presbyterian Church at Allentown, served with Witherspoon in Presbytery meetings, and invited Witherspoon to preach at important Allentown Church events.[34] In February 1777, John Witherspoon wrote his son David, "I . . . find that by Mr. Montgomery's care, not many of my books are gone, and but little of the standing furniture is destroyed."[35]

Thomas Stockton (1730-1799)

Thomas Stockton was a first cousin of Richard Stockton, Sr., (the signer of the Declaration of Independence) and the leading

---

33. Thomas Harrison Montgomery, *A Genealogical History of the Family of Montgomery* (H.B. Ashmead, 1863), 110.

34. F. Dean Storms, *History of Allentown Presbyterian Church, Allentown, New Jersey, 1720-1970* (Allentown Messenger, 1970), 60, 67-68.

35. John Witherspoon to David Witherspoon, February 12, 1777, in Paul Hubert Smith, *Letters of Delegates to Congress* (Library of Congress, 1980), vol. 6, 269.

general merchant in the village of Princeton.[36] He owned a farm on the Rocky Hill-Pennington Road east of Silus's tavern. Silus Watters' father-in-law, William Savidge, Sr., was overseer of the road "from the Province Line east to Thomas Stockton's land."[37]

Like others in Princeton, Thomas filed a damage claim for losses in the war including a destroyed cedar barn, fencing, pork, flax, potatoes, hay, and damage to his house.[38] During all of 1777, Stockton was commissary for the makeshift military hospital in Nassau Hall, providing food, wine, and spirits for the sick. In 1782, he served on a committee in Princeton to organize an Association to Prevent Trade and Intercourse with the Enemy, along with James Moore and Daniel Slack, another signer at Silus Watters' parties.[39]

When Congress met at Princeton in the summer and fall of 1783, Thomas Stockton super-stocked his store and stretched every nerve to supply the exacting tastes of the delegates, providing such choice perishables as limes and pineapples.[40] A loyal member of the Presbyterian Church, in 1784 he and James Moore were among the most generous of fifty-two signers who pledged to refurbish the war-damaged building.[41]

---

36. Thomas was the son of Robert Stockton (born 1678). Richard (the signer) was the son of Robert's brother Richard Stockton (born 1693).

37. David Blackwell email to J. Lawrence Brasher, March 25, 2018.

38. Thomas Stockton Damage Claim, Inventories of Damages by the British and Americans in New Jersey, 1776-1782, New Jersey State Archives.

39. Hageman, *Princeton,* I, 280.

40. Varnum Lansing Collins, *The Continental Congress at Princeton* (Princeton: The University Library, 1908), 255-258.

41. Hageman, *Princeton*, II, 88.

Joseph Leigh (1749-1823) and Ichabod Leigh, Jr. (1750-?)

Ichabod Leigh was a Chosen Freeholder, Tax Assessor, and on the Town Committee of the Western Precinct.[42] Joseph Leigh was a customer at James Moore's tannery in 1800.[43] In 1784, he pledged with Thomas Stockton and James Moore to rebuild the Presbyterian Church.[44] Brothers Joseph and Ichabod Leigh also had brothers Daniel (1762-1823) and Zebulon (1763-?), the latter two were Silus Watters' brothers-in-law. Zebulon married Silus Watters' sister-in-law Hannah Savidge (1767-1833), and Daniel married Silus Watters' sister Phebe Watters (1748-1821).

Joseph Leigh was a tailor and lived in town on the east side of Witherspoon Street not far from James Moore's house on Nassau Street. It may have been Leigh who punched and sewed the makeshift repair securing the silver top mount to the leather scabbard of James Moore's dog-head sword. As well as supporting the Presbyterian Church, Joseph Leigh helped found the Princeton Firefighters Company in 1788 and the Princeton Academy in 1790 along with James Moore and another neighbor near the corner of Nassau and Witherspoon streets, silversmith Samuel Stout, Jr. After Stout's early death in 1796, Joseph Leigh helped Stout's widow, Helena Cruser Stout, administer Samuel's estate.[45] Samuel Stout, Jr., was also a second cousin of the four Leigh brothers. The mother of the four, Anne Stout Leigh (1724-1776), who married

---

42. Snell, *Hunterdon and Somerset*, 841-843.

43. Moore, "Account book," 50.

44. Hageman, *Princeton*, II, 88.

45. Inventory of Samuel Stout, Jr. Aaron Mattison and Stephen Morford also assisted with the inventory. Williams, *Silversmiths*, 113.

Ichabod Leigh, Sr., in 1744, was the niece of Samuel Stout, Jr.,'s grandfather Samuel Stout (1709-1781).

Silus Watters' brother-in-law Daniel Leigh served in the militia with Watters for two stints under James Moore. Sixteen years after Silus Watters moved over thirty miles north to Lebanon Township, where he operated a distillery, he delivered to Daniel Leigh in Princeton "one barrel of cider and seven gallons of spirits."[46]

Zebulon Stout (1723-1814)

Zebulon Stout was the uncle of Ichabod, Joseph, Daniel, and Zebulon Leigh. Their mother, Anne Stout Leigh (1724-1776), was Zebulon's sister. Zebulon Stout was a first cousin once removed of Samuel Stout, Jr., the silversmith. At the time of Silus's 1789 party, Zebulon was a Chosen Freeholder.[47] During the war, he served on the Western Precinct Town Committee.

The Stouts were founders of the Hopewell Baptist Church, and Zebulon and his father, Captain Zebulon Bollen Stout (1699-1785), were leaders of the congregation. They and Anne Stout Leigh were at church Sunday morning, April 23, 1775, when news arrived of the fighting at Lexington. When the Sunday meeting let out, they heard fellow church member Joab Houghton, standing on the horse-mounting block, make his legendary churchyard appeal: "Who follows me to Boston?" Church member John Hart later signed the Declaration of Independence.[48]

---

46. "Silus Watters Appel Book," November 1808, Watters Papers.

47. Snell, *Hunterdon and Somerset*, 841-843.

48. Ege, *Pioneers*, 19.

Nicholas Golden [Goulder] (1723-?)

The Goldens were one of the first families to settle in Hopewell in the early eighteenth century. About 1762, Nicholas Golden built a substantial house, still extant, in the Western Precinct just east of the Great Road a mile from Silus Watters' tavern.[49] He purchased 92 acres from his friend Samuel Tucker (1721-1789) of Trenton. Tucker was a member of the first Committee of Correspondence in Trenton in July 1774, and later Vice President and Treasurer of the Provincial Congress. In May 1775, he voted with the Congress to organize and arm a militia in response to the news of Lexington.[50] When the British advanced on Trenton in December 1776, he hid the treasury of the Congress at the house of John Abbott in Trenton.

It was at the home of Nicholas Golden in May 1778, that twenty-four Somerset freeholders, including Henry Berrien, Joseph Stryker, and William Savidge, Sr., met to determine the fate of deceased loyalist Joseph Stockton's property. In 1779, Nicholas billed the Continental Army for services in carting supplies.[51]

Nicholas's cousin Abraham Golden was a member of Captain John Stryker's Light Horse Troop of the Somerset County Militia. Napping at home after returning from a Light Horse scouting party, Abraham was captured by a band of Hessians, along with his sixteen-year-old relative, Jacob Lane Golden, known as "little Jake." Although small—the size of a twelve-year-old—Jake was a precocious giant in the use of profanity. The Hessians hustled

---

49. Brecknell, *Montgomery Township*, 77.

50. Snell, *Hunterdon and Somerset*, 27-31.

51. "Certificates issued at Princeton by Robert Stockton, Q.M., 1779-1780," in Dorothy Agans Stratford, *Certificates and Receipts of Revolutionary New Jersey* (Lambertville: Hunterdon House), vol. II, 204.

Abraham, Jake, and others to Princeton, all the while enduring insulting verbal volleys from little Jake. At Nassau Hall, the prisoners were inspected by a British colonel, who, when he came to Jake, asked the Hession sergeant why he had brought "that dirty-nosed little brat," and told Jake to run home to his mother, which he did.[52] Abraham, not so fortunate, was sent to a prison in New York City and died there within a year.

Aaron Mattison (1723-1800)

A quartermaster for the Army, Aaron Mattison was a neighbor in town of James Moore, Joseph Leigh, and Samuel Stout, Jr. Aaron assisted Joseph Leigh in taking the inventory of Stout's effects for his widow, Helena.[53] Along with Moore and others, Mattison pledged to restore the Presbyterian Church in 1784, and he contributed with Moore to the opening of the Princeton Academy in 1790.[54] Perhaps Aaron Mattison's most important role in the war was as College Steward of Nassau Hall (see chapter 5). He was present at, or shortly after, the Battle of Princeton, when the British fled into the building in a last-ditch attempt to hold off the Americans, and when James Moore broke open the door. Nassau Hall remained Aaron Mattison's responsibility when it transformed into both a prison, with inmates overseen by James Moore, and into a military hospital, immediately after the Battle of Princeton through at least 1780. He had his hands full as the appointed coffin maker for the hospital. A typhus epidemic raged

52. Ege, *Pioneers*, 31-33.

53. Inventory of Samuel Stout, Jr.

54. Hageman, *Princeton,* II, 88.

in the summer of 1778, and after the Battle of Monmouth, the hospital received the injured whose wounds had not been dressed for two weeks. Joseph Scudder, a college student who boarded at Mattison's house, saw "numbers of [coffins] piled up in the college entry." At Scudder's graduation in 1778, held in Nassau Hall, a large portion of the audience were convalescent soldiers.[55]

Daniel Slack (1741-1811)

Daniel Slack attended both parties. Surely at these Christmas get-togethers he regaled the group of friends with his family's stories of Washington's crossing the Delaware Christmas night 1776 at Slack's Ferry (a.k.a. Johnson's Ferry) to surprise Trenton. Daniel's father, James Slack (1706-1791), and his brother Richard (1733-?) ran the ferry on the Jersey side of the river. In the wind, sleet, and snow, the Slacks muscled the flat boats against the current and ice floes and floated 400 tons of cannons and wagons and a hundred horses to the New Jersey riverbank. The cannons were the decisive factor in the victory at Trenton.

Daniel Slack lived on Silus Watters' road, owned 201 acres, and was overseer of the road from the Province Line to Rocky Hill in 1779-1780, the same year that James Moore served the community as overseer of the road from Weston to Kingston.[56] In 1782, Slack met at Beekman's Tavern with James Moore, Thomas Stockton, and Dr. John Witherspoon, Jr., to form the Association to Prevent Trade and Intercourse with the Enemy. The committee drafted a bill to be

---

55. Mary C. Gillett, *The Army Medical Department, 1775-1818* (Washington, DC: Center of Military History, 2004), 99, 110.

56. Snell, *Hunterdon and Somerset*, 841-843.

signed by area residents "not to purchase or wear imported goods of British manufacture" and "to bring violators of the law to justice."[57]

Joseph Stryker (1743-1800)

Baptized at the Harlingen Dutch Reformed Church, Joseph Stryker owned a farm of 67 acres in the Western Precinct. He was with Henry Berrien and William Savidge, Sr., at the 1782 meeting at Nicholas Golden's house to decide the fate of the property of deceased loyalist Joseph Stockton. In 1783, he petitioned for payment for military service in the Revolution. A member of the Western Precinct Town Committee 1787-1791, Joseph enjoyed taverns. He signed Somerset licenses for four taverns in addition to that of Silus Watters.[58]

Isaac Stryker (1751-1817)

Also a member of the Harlingen Dutch Reformed Church, Isaac Stryker owned a farm of 253 acres in the Western Precinct and was a private in the Revolutionary War.[59]

John Roberson

John Roberson was a longtime friend of Silus Watters from their youth in Maidenhead. He and Watters served together in the fall of 1777 in the company of Watters' cousin Captain Philip Phillips of the First Regiment, Hunterdon County Militia. Their second lieutenant was Elias Hunt, who was pursued by the Hessian Jaeger

---

57. Dr. John Witherspoon, Jr., was a medical doctor, Princeton class of 1779, who was lost at sea in 1795. Hageman, *Princeton*, I, 179-180.

58. Hageman, *Princeton*, I, 175; William Stryker, email to J. Lawrence Brasher, September 6, 2018.

59. William Stryker, email to J. Lawrence Brasher, September 6, 2018.

on horseback. Silus Watters was a corporal and John Roberson a private. In 1790, John Roberson was living in the Western Precinct as a "householder," which meant that he owned no land there.[60]

John Scott (? - ?)

John Scott served in James Moore's militia company. He owned 56 acres in the Western Precinct and was a cooper. How fitting that he was at the party, since he may have rived the barrels and casks that held the tavern's cider and spirits.[61]

Abraham Voorhees (1765-1822)

Abraham Voorhees served in James Moore's militia company. He was at both parties at Silus Watters' and was a customer of James Moore's tannery in 1800, barter-paid by Moore with tanned hides and skins.[62] His farm of 147 acres joined his father John's farm along the north branch of Bedens Brook southeast of Blawenburg. He is buried at the Kingston Presbyterian Church.[63]

Benjamin Hunt (1758-?)

Benjamin Hunt served in James Moore's militia company. He was a customer of James Moore's tannery in 1800, also paid by Moore in tanned hides and skins. He was a single man with no land in 1790.[64]

---

60. Muster Roll No. 689, New Jersey State Archives.

61. Scott, Voorhees, Benjamin and Varnell Hunt are listed in James Moore's militia class list October 24, 1777, Manuscript 1500, New Jersey State Archives.

62. Moore, "Account Book," 24.

63. Snell, *Hunterdon and Somerset*, 837.

64. Moore, "Account Book," 30.

Varnell [Varnal] Hunt (1760-?)

Varnell Hunt served in James Moore's militia company. He attended Silus's party with his brother, Benjamin. He owned a farm of 90 acres in the Western Precinct. He and his brother were distant cousins of Silus Watters through Silus's maternal great-grandmother Sarah Hunt, who married Silas Titus (1677-1748) in 1715.

Jeremiah Van Dyke (1749-1826)

Jeremiah Van Dyke owned a farm of 100 acres, possibly near the other Van Dykes along the north branch of Bedens Brook.

Richard [Ryck] Sutfin [Sutphen] (1751-?)

Richard Sutfin owned a farm of 187 acres in the Western Precinct. He was the son of Aert and Janettye Van Meter Sutfin.

Timothy Baker (? - ?)

Timothy Baker owned a farm of 100 acres in the Western Precinct.

Enoch Elberson (? - ?)

Enoch Elberson owned a farm of 46 acres in the Western Precinct.

Garret Van Pelt (? - ?)

Garret Van Pelt owned a farm of 79 acres in the Western Precinct.

The Christmas party patrons of Silus's tavern, in the words of folklorist Daniel Patterson, "lived in interlinked networks of kindred, neighbors, and fellow members of churches and militia companies. They served on juries and on court-ordered teams to repair roads in their neighborhoods. They made music and entertained each other with gossip and stories. They married, and they buried their kin."[65] These thick family and social ties, including many and diverse connections to James Moore who was part of the community, confirm that Moore not only grew up with Silus Watters and became his militia captain, but also he remained a perennial presence in the life of Watters after the war. For Silus, his own war experience, some of it shared with Moore, and tavern tales of battles, heroes, hardship, and humor eventually coalesced in James Moore's dog-head sword, an icon of memories, a "relick connected with incidents on which the soul delights to dwell."[66]

———

Not long after the holiday parties, in 1792 Silus Watters and his family left Princeton and the tavern and purchased a farm thirty miles north on Schooley's Mountain in Lebanon Township, Hunterdon County. Although the tavern had the support of friends and neighbors, the tavern house belonged to Sarah Watters' parents, William and Elizabeth Savidge. Probably opened by Watters at the close of the war, the house was located considerably and somewhat inconveniently south of the actual road and could not compete with long-established multiple public houses at

65. Daniel W, Patterson, *The True Image: Gravestone Art and the Culture of Scotch Irish Settlers in the Pennsylvania and Carolina Backcountry* (Chapel Hill: University of North Carolina Press, 2012), 58.

66. Boudreau and Lovell, *A Material World*, 294.

nearby crossroads villages of Pennington and Hopewell.[67] Silus's wife, Sarah, was one of eleven children, all potential heirs, so there was little chance that Silus and Sarah would inherit enough of her parents' farm to support themselves. Living with Sarah's parents, Sarah and Silus already had four children by 1792. They needed space and a farm of their own.[68]

Silus Watters purchased three hundred thirty-five acres in Lebanon for three hundred forty-two pounds, eleven shillings, and two pence in gold and silver.[69] The farm had been advertised for sale in the *New York Journal* as early as 1772 by three trustees of the estate of Quaker John Sykes of Bordentown, but the war had intervened. Silus had his eye on the property for many years before he bought it. The newspaper described the farm, which was the highest cultivated land—over one thousand feet—in Hunterdon County: "two log houses, other buildings, the land good for grass or wheat, 60 or 70 acres of plowland cleared, a young orchard, 8 or 10 acres of meadow cleared, 40 or 50 acres of swamp to clear, and a woodland well-timbered and watered, within 2 or 3 miles of Change Water and Point Forges and several grist mills. . . . Its being so near said Iron-works, makes the timber valuable, as the purchaser may fell the timber standing."[70]

---

67. Alice Blackwell Lewis, *Hopewell Valley Heritage* (Hopewell: The Hopewell Museum, 1973), 15; Map, William Savidge, Sr., estate papers, 175ff.

68. Chambers, *Early Germans*, 355-356.

69. West Jersey Deed Book, A-Q, 474-476.

70. *The New York Journal; or The General Advertiser*, No. 1521, February 27, 1772, in William Nelson, ed., *Extracts from American Newspapers, Relating to New Jersey*, vol. IX, 1772-1773, (Paterson, NJ: The Call Printing Co., 1916), 64.

Joseph Hilborn, a merchant in Philadelphia, friend of Benjamin Franklin, and the sole surviving trustee twenty years after the farm was first advertised, took back a mortgage from Silus Watters. Two years later Silus paid it off financed by the sale of 100 acres to his widowed mother, Priscilla Titus Watters, who moved there from Hopewell after her father, Ephraim Titus (1696-1789), died.[71] Priscilla Watters' daughter and son-in-law, Martha and William Morgan, Sr., came with her and leased her new Lebanon "plantation."

Silus saw the young orchard and the well-watered land as opportunity to continue his expertise in distilling. His 1806 manuscript "Appel Book" testifies to a brisk business in making cider, applejack, peach brandy, and whiskey for his neighbors in Lebanon.[72] The extensive wheat fields of his farm produced a market crop, and in 1808, his cousin Governor Joseph Bloomfield appointed him Justice of the Peace. He was a founder of the nearby log Pleasant Grove Presbyterian Church.[73]

Silus Watters died on his farm at age sixty-nine during the first cutting of hay in 1820. His inventory listed "stills, cisterns, hogsheads, and barrels," and numerous debtors who owed his estate nearly a thousand dollars.[74] His funeral was preached by the first settled pastor of the "Grove Church," an Ulster-born Scot,

---

71. Hunterdon County Mortgage Book 1, 523-524; Hunterdon County Deed Book 11, 365-367.

72. Silus Watters, "Appel Book," 1806-1808, Watters Papers.

73. The Pleasant Grove Presbyterian Church was first recognized by the New Brunswick Presbytery in 1806, but a log church had been established there some time before that. W.W. Munsell, *History of Morris County, New Jersey* (New York: George Macnamara, 1882), 387.

74. Hunterdon County Estate Papers, No. 3103, New Jersey State Archives.

The Rev. Joseph Campbell, who was an honorary 1806 graduate of Princeton. Watters' headstone and footstone displayed some of the finest workmanship in the churchyard.[75] At the top of the sophisticated headstone his name was carved "Silas Watters, Esq."

Figure 42. The footstone with initials SW and the reverse of the headstone of Silus Watters (1751-1820), Pleasant Grove Presbyterian Church Cemetery, Washington Township, Morris County, New Jersey.

---

75. The fallen pieces of the inscription, rescued by Nancy Dontzin in the 1970s, are preserved by David and Sue Tullo of Lebanon Township.

CHAPTER 8

Moment and Maker

The "shot heard 'round the world" at the Battle of Lexington on April 19, 1775, touched off a flurry of militia preparations in New Jersey. Such words as Joab Houghton's churchyard appeal to his fellow Hopewell Baptists, "Who follows me to Boston?" spurred men to form voluntary, unofficial militia companies determined to defend their rights.[1] As early as February 1774, in response to the Boston Tea Party and the blockade of the port by the British, the New Jersey House of Assembly had resolved to set up a "Standing Committee of Correspondence," and soon after, individual counties, including Somerset and Hunterdon, set up their own committees to elect representatives to a Provincial Congress to meet at Trenton.[2] On July 4, 1774, the Somerset committee, including John Witherspoon, declared opposition to

---

1. Ralph Ege, *Pioneers of Old Hopewell* (Hopewell: Hopewell Museum, 1963), 19; Cone, Edward W. and Spencer Cone, *Some Account of the Life of Spencer Houghton Cone: A Baptist Preacher in America* (New York: Livermore and Rudd, 1856), 12.

2. "Somerset Patriotism Preceding the Revolutionary War," *Somerset County Historical Quarterly*, vol. 5, no. 4 (October 1916): 241-244.

taxation without representation and pledged relief to "the poor and helpless" citizens of Boston. In December, the Freeholders chose representatives to serve on Committees of Inspection to patrol their townships to find anyone who did not "oppose the arbitrary and cruel measures of the British Ministry." In May 1775, the Somerset committee resolved to join with other counties to arm and support a new militia.[3]

The Militia Act required all men from ages sixteen to fifty immediately to form into companies in each township. Each man was to "furnish himself with a good musket or firelock and bayonet, sword, or tomahawk."[4] The date of 1775 inscribed on the dog-head sword scabbard's top mount nicely fits with James Moore's purchase of a sword at that time. Armorers and silversmiths in Trenton and Philadelphia were hard pressed to supply enough militia weapons quickly, and they hired extra journeymen to work late hours to meet the feverish demand.[5] In August, Philemon Dickinson, soon to be Major General of the New Jersey Militia, bought a silver-hilted sword from Trenton silversmith John Fitch. Fitch also was busy repairing guns and making bayonets, silver-mounted cuttoe scabbards, regimental buttons, and tools for cleaning gun barrels.[6]

---

3. "Somerset Patriotism," 245.

4. "New Jersey Militia: Heard's Brigade," http://www.newjerseymilitia.org /history.htm.

5. In 1775, Trenton silversmith John Fitch employed seven journeymen. Harold E. Gillingham, "John Fitch, Jack of Many Trades," *The Magazine Antiques* (February 1939): 73; Account Book of Thomas Shields, Winterthur Library, Fol. 27.

6. John Fitch Account Book, August 24, 1775.

The events of summer 1775 stirred the colonies into what was called a popular *rage militaire,* in which new militia companies formed to defend citizen rights. Philip Fithian, the young New Jersey Presbyterian minister, protégé of John Witherspoon, acquaintance of James Moore, and soon to be militia chaplain, summed up the excitement that he saw that summer: "Battalions of Militia & Minute-Men embodying—Drums & Fife rattling— Military Language in every Mouth—Numbers who . . . were plain Countrymen have now clothed themselves in martial forms—Powdered Hair and Sharp pinched Beavers—Uniforms in Dress with their battalion—Swords on their thighs—& stern in the Art of War—Resolved in steady manly Firmness to support & establish American Liberty or die in Battle!"[7]

Unmarked swords from the Revolution are attributed to a maker by similarities to marked swords and by region of provenance, if known. The handful of extant marked dog-headed swords were made by Ephraim Brasher, by John Bailey and his partner James Youle, all working in New York City, and by David Hall in Philadelphia. One of the Brasher swords belonged to Ethan Allen. The finest known Bailey dog-head sword was made for Revolutionary Captain Isaac Roosevelt (1726-1794), great-great grandfather of Franklin Roosevelt.[8]

Curators and collectors who have examined the dog-head sword have noticed its similarities in style to those made by John Bailey and, in one instance, to the dog-headed sword by David

---

7. Albion, Greenhalgh, and Dodson, *Philip Vickers Fithia*n, 131.

8. The Allen sword was part of the Lattimer Collection at Fort Ticonderoga; the Roosevelt sword is in the H. Kels Swan Collection at The Museum of the American Revolution at Washington's Crossing, New Jersey.

Hall. But they agree that the details of this sword uniquely differ from others and that it probably did not come from either Bailey or Hall. Although the general form of the hilt is like those of Bailey and other silver hilts popular at the start of the Revolution, it is dissimilar to Bailey swords in these respects: The shape of the dog head is different. The engraving on the head, guard, and ferrules is different. The engraving on the guard is less roundly foliate and floral; it is more angular. The feathered edge pattern on the guard is different. No other swords display the figure of a saltire in a roundel, as presented on the guard, and most of the guard engraving is deeply incised, or bright-cut. The leaf-tip and cross-hatching designs on the lower ferrule are not found on swords by Bailey. The upper stud to hold the chain guard is attached under the dog's chin instead of held in the teeth as on those by Bailey and all other dog-heads. Curators believe the blade to be of American manufacture, and Bailey's blades are not.[9] Finally, the stitching of the leather scabbard is less fine and regular than that of the Roosevelt-Bailey sword, and the scabbard contains an extra strip of joining leather in the middle from the top to the tip.[10]

---

9. Andrew F. Lustyik, "John Bailey, Swordmaker," *The Gun Report* (February 1980): 12-14.

10. Curators and collectors who have handled or seen photographs of the sword and noted resemblance to Bailey's work include collector John K. Lattimer, Charles Montgomery of the Yale University Art Museum, Harold Peterson, and Ann Wagner of Winterthur Museum; also Daniel Hartzler, John Dubozy, and H. Kels Swan. John Lattimer x-rayed the sword with several other dog-heads to see the interior construction, and discovered similarities between the tang of this sword (the interior extension of the blade into the hilt) and that of the Hall sword, but all of the exterior decorative details are different. Perhaps the blades are from the same source.

James Moore likely purchased the sword from Trenton silversmith John Fitch (1743-1798), whose journeymen included Silus Watters' friend from Hopewell and Princeton, young Samuel Stout, Jr., a recent apprentice of notable Philadelphia silversmith Thomas Shields (1743-1819). Stout left his apprenticeship with Shields to work with Fitch in Trenton in early 1775. In 1776, he was ready to open his own shop in Princeton, but the war made him wait. His family tradition claims that he already had been working "at the jewelry trade" in Princeton since 1775. Stout mentions his own set of tools stored at home in Hopewell in a letter to his parents in 1776.[11] It is possible that Stout made the sword hilt and scabbard by himself in Princeton or Hopewell. The sword might have been mounted while Stout was with Thomas Shields in Philadelphia, but Fitch's shop is more probable. Both stylistic clues and commercial, political, and social networks point to Stout and Fitch in Trenton.

Born in Windsor, Connecticut, John Fitch abandoned an unhappy marriage there and arrived in Trenton in May 1769. In the 1780s, encouraged by James Moore's former militia captain William Churchhill Houston, Fitch invented the first steamboat, which carried passengers on the Delaware between Philadelphia and Trenton.[12] Within a few months after locating in Trenton and working for a tinsmith, he purchased the next-door shop and tools of silversmith John Wilson whose drinking had ruined his business. In a year, Fitch's trade was so extensive that he hired several journeymen silversmiths and clock makers. His 1773-1776 account book, even with many missing pages, lists a

---

11. Ege, *Pioneers*, 267.

12. McLachan, *Princetonians*, 643-647.

prodigious output of 1 coffeepot, 20 cream pitchers, 8 tankards, 26 cans, 277 tablespoons, 651 teaspoons, 2 porringers, over 500 silver and brass buttons, camp cups, sugar tongs, marrow spoons, pap spoons, and many sword mountings and gun repairs.[13] Fitch reported that he regularly traveled the New Jersey countryside in a twenty-mile radius of Trenton peddling silver and mending clocks and watches. He boasted: "I believe I soon got a greater run of business than any silversmith in Philadelphia, or at least it was the opinion of my journeymen I had."[14]

In 1776, the New Jersey Committee of Safety chose Fitch as official gunsmith and armorer for the State of New Jersey, a task he filled until the Battle of Trenton, when the British army ransacked his shop. In 1775 and early 1776, John Fitch, Samuel Stout, and his six other journeymen were pressed with so many orders for swords, guns, and bayonets that they worked nights and on Sundays. The Trenton Methodists, whom Fitch had recently joined, expelled him for profaning the Sabbath.[15]

In spite of Fitch's prolific production of silver pieces and military equipment, very few examples of his work remain. In 1949, historian of New Jersey silver Carl Williams reported that "there are known only two cream pots, seven tablespoons, two teaspoons, and a pair of sugar tongs bearing the mark of John Fitch."[16] Since then, little other Fitch silver has come to light.

---

13. John Fitch Account Book.

14. John Fitch's Journal, Ridgway Library, Philadelphia, 44.

15. Thomas Westcott, *The Life of John Fitch, the Inventor of the Steamboat* (Philadelphia: J.B. Lippincott, 1857), 58-59.

16. Carl M. Williams, *Silversmiths of New Jersey, 1700-1825* (Philadelphia: George S. MacManus Company, 1949), 132. For the best accounts of Fitch as

None of his many silver-hilted swords is known. Years of searching for the silver hilt that he fashioned in August 1775 for the famous and wealthy General Philemon Dickinson of Trenton, for comparison to this sword, have proved fruitless.[17]

In 1775, after three years of training in Philadelphia with Thomas Shields, Samuel Stout, Jr., returned home to work for John Fitch. Samuel's numerous prominent family members and his local social connections drew business for Fitch, but in 1776 Stout joined Captain Joab Houghton's Company, Heard's Brigade, First Regiment, Hunterdon County.[18] He was taken prisoner at the Battle of Long Island, August 27, 1776, and consigned to a vile New York prison for three months. Word of mouth and a series of letters from his friends kept his parents in Hopewell in suspense. They first presumed him dead, then missing, then perhaps a prisoner. Awakened at eleven at night the day after the battle, Samuel's parents heard the news that "thousands were killed on both sides." On August 29, Samuel, Sr., reported a "general

---

silversmith, see Williams, *Silversmiths*, 130-138, and Gillingham, "John Fitch: Jack of Many Trades,": 73-75. Peterson in *The American Sword*, 245, states, "A naval dirk bearing his mark is known." Current attempts to locate it have failed.

17. John Fitch Account Book, August 24, 1775.

18. On June 16, 1772, Stout contracted to work for Shields for five years and three months. He left Shields for Fitch before his contract expired. Catherine B. Hollan, *Philadelphia Silversmiths and Related Artisans to 1861* (Hollan Press, 2013), 184. Stout was part of one of the largest extended Hunterdon/Somerset families, all descended from the legendary Penelope Stout (1622-1732?) of Monmouth County, who survived shipwreck and scalping on the New Jersey coast. She afterward bore ten children, and allegedly lived to be 110. At the time of her death, two generations before Samuel Stout's silversmith career, she reportedly already had over 500 descendants. Frank R. Stockton, *Stories of New Jersey* (New York: American Book Company, 1896), 57-68.

mourning in ye neighborhood." On September 1, he received a letter saying his son and Zephaniah Stout were missing and thought possibly taken prisoner. On September 13, Gideon Lyon, Silus Watters' brother-in-law returning from the defeat of Fort Washington in New York, reported that Samuel, Jr., had not been heard of.

When Samuel was released from prison, he wrote his parents on December 4, 1776: "Honored Father and Mother, I take this opportunity to let you know that I am in good health and that I have got out of prison and have got to work at my trade. I long to see you but I cannot come yet as I have engaged to stay two or three months with Mr. Reeves the Golde Smith with whom I have to work. I have been a prisoner from August 27 to Novem. 24 and in that time I suffered more than I can express. I long to hear from you. I expect matters will be made up soon and we will once more have peace. I have just heard that the Kings Troops are at Trenton. I think it best to stay here part or all of this winter as my work is very plenty in New York. I was almost naked when I got to work but hope with God's blessing to be able to have some good clothes in a short time. Give my respects to all my friends. Write to me the first opportunity. Please take care of my tools. If it is God's will I intend to use them once more."[19]

---

19. Ege, *Pioneers*, 264-267. Stephen Reeves (1738-1778?) was a master silversmith who grew up in Burlington County, New Jersey, and was a boyhood friend of Philip Fithian. He worked in Philadelphia until 1774, when he divorced his wife in disputes over his loyalist sentiments. He probably knew Samuel Stout in Philadelphia when Stout worked for Thomas Shields. Reeves fled to loyalist New York in 1776 and was there to employ Stout when Stout was released from prison. "Philadelphia Silversmiths, Additions and Corrections (December 2013)," www.catherinehollan.com/_Addns_Dec_2013.pdf.

In 1779, Samuel Stout, Jr., opened his own shop in Princeton, where he worked until his early death in 1795. Like Fitch, only a few items of Stout's silver survive, including a teaspoon and a pierced sugar tongs, or "tea tongs." The current location of the tongs is unknown.[20]

Thomas Shields, Stout's first teacher, conducted his silversmith business from several locations on Front Street, Philadelphia, from 1765-1791. Many examples of his work survive. Although there are no known extant silver-hilted swords from Shields, his shop, too, was doing a brisk business supplying them. Like Fitch, whose silver sword mountings first showed in his accounts in July 1775, especially in 1775 and early 1776, Shields was silver mounting many hunting swords, repairing and upgrading old ones, and offering the full complement of swords, scabbards, and belts. Shields also supplied Fitch with some materials, but no complete swords. Juliet Chase, in her study of Shields, notes that his sales relied heavily on kinship ties and word-of-mouth. In fact, Shields sold some of his silver to prominent Somerset and Hunterdon County, New Jersey, residents. These included the signers Richard Stockton of Princeton and John Hart of Hopewell.[21]

Fitch's clients also came to him through word-of-mouth, kinship ties, and regional trade routes. Like the thick ropes that moored the Durham boats to the Trenton docks, hundreds of commercial and social connections tethered Somerset, Hunterdon, and Monmouth citizens to Trenton and to Fitch's work.

20. Williams, *Silversmiths*, 109-117. Since 1949, the tongs have passed to an unknown owner. Personal conversation with H. Kels Swan, summer 2014.

21. Julia Chase, "A Prospectus for Thomas Shields, Goldsmith, Philadelphia," May 17, 1995, Winterthur Library, Fol. 27; Thomas Shields Daybook, 1775-1791, Winterthur Library, Fol. 27.

Residents of west central and central New Jersey went to market, to political gatherings, and to court at Trenton.

John Fitch's account book, unfortunately with many tantalizing missing pages, provides a sample of the widespread—as far away as Piscataway, New Jersey—and prosperous customers of his silver, swords, guns, and bayonets: Major General Philemon Dickinson of Trenton—a silver-mounted sword; Andrew Morgan of Hopewell—silver buckles; Philip Phillips of Maidenhead, captain of Silus Watters' militia company and guide for Washington's Trenton victory—a bayonet and cleaning a gun; Sergeant John Phillips, Philip's cousin and guide for Washington at Trenton; Captain John Mott, grist mill owner and guide for Washington at Trenton; Elias Hunt of Maidenhead, who was pursued on horseback by the Hessian jaeger and saved by a hidden picket who shot the jaeger near the Maidenhead church;[22] Rensselaer Williams, Justice of the Peace, who ran a public house at Trenton Ferry; [23] Lieutenant Colonel Abraham Hunt, who in his cozy Trenton home entertained the unsuspecting Hessian Colonel Rahl on the night of Washington's crossing.[24]

The best evidence of the sword's origin with Fitch and Stout is the sword itself—tangible clues. The most telling, mentioned earlier in the description of the sword, is the distinctive feathered

---

22. David Hackett Fischer, *Washington's Crossing* (New York: Oxford University Press, 2003), 295.

23. "Trenton Historical Society," http://www.Trentonhistory.org/Documents /manuscript/MS1173.html; "Information about Phillip Phillips," http://www .genealogy.com.

24. Larry Kidder, "Guiding Washington to Trenton," *Journal of the American Revolution*, May 6, 2014, http://allthingsliberty.com/2014/05/guiding -washington-to-trenton/.

edge pattern on the guard—a "skewed herringbone"—parallel right-angle cuts to a center line with opposing parallel cuts at a slant to the center line. One curator describes it as "'gadrooning' that is morphing into a 'feathered edge'."[25] The design is angular and geometric rather than foliate. (See figures 18, 19, 20.)

Similar decoration appears on no other known silver object of the period except one—sugar tongs made several years later by Samuel Stout, Jr., in his Princeton shop.[26] The side edges of Stout's sugar tongs bear the same skewed herringbone pattern that is on the sword guard. Stout worked for Fitch, and possibly also in Princeton, for most of 1775, the date on the sword. None of the more numerous extant works of Stout's former employer Thomas Shields displays this design. Stout himself may have created the novel pattern that appears on the sword while working for Fitch or on his own in Princeton, or Fitch perhaps used it on his own work, and Stout learned it from him.

A second similarity between the sword and the tongs are pairs of chasing marks that resemble quotation marks in print. They repeatedly appear on the nose, cheeks, and jowls of the sword's dog head (figure 16), and the same marks appear around the script initials and next to the feathered edge on Stout's sugar tongs.

Finally, the design on the sword guard of a saltire, an X-shape, highlighted in the center of swirling rays appears on no other

25. Ann Wagner, Associate Curator of Decorative Arts, Winterthur Museum, email message to J. Lawrence Brasher, March 26, 2015.

26. Williams, *Silversmiths*, 112; Ann Wagner, email message to J. Lawrence Brasher, May 8, 2015. I have searched unsuccessfully for other examples of the pattern.

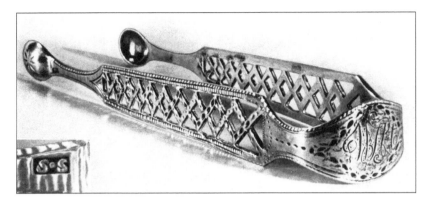

Figure 43. Sugar tongs by Samuel Stout, Jr., with the skewed herringbone pattern along the sides and pairs of chasing marks near the script initials and the edge. From Williams, *Silversmiths of New Jersey.*

known silver of the period. Its unique figure lessens the possibility of makers other than Fitch and Stout.[27] (figure 20.)

John Fitch and Samuel Stout probably procured their American steel blades right in Trenton. By the 1770s, Trenton steel was highly regarded and sold in Philadelphia and New York. A June 1772 advertisement in the *New York Gazette* announced that

Figure 44. Detail of the skewed herringbone pattern on Stout's sugar tongs.

---

27. Ann Wagner, email message to J. Lawrence Brasher, May 8, 2015.

Bowne and Rickman had "American steel manufactured by John Zane at Trentown, esteemed quite equal, if not better in quality than what is imported from England."[28] In March 1773, Philadelphia merchant John Pemberton was selling "steel manufactured at Trenton, either in the blister, or neatly drawn and fagotted; also in thin plates for springs and mill saws."[29]

28. *New York Gazette*, June 15, 1772, 4.

29. *The Pennsylvania Packet*, March 15, 1773, 3; Larry Kidder, email message to J. Lawrence Brasher, July 3, 2015.

CHAPTER 9

Iconography

The sword held symbolic importance both for its original maker and owner and for its subsequent caretakers. Over time it evoked multiple meanings, from its silver designs probably chosen by James Moore and Samuel Stout, Jr., in 1775, to its rescue from the family farm auction by my grandfather Lawrence Watters in 1918. Its iconography reflected various histories according to who viewed it.

On July 3, 1775, on Cambridge Common, General George Washington drew his sword from its scabbard and formally took command of the Continental Army.[1] Symbolizing the people's determination to defend themselves against all enemies, Washington's first national gesture, publicized throughout the colonies, inspired, along with the 1775 militia acts, the flurry of orders for swords from John Fitch and Thomas Shields that began midsummer in 1775.

---

1. Alfred F. Hopkins, "Some American Military Swords," *The Regional Review*, vol. IV, no. 1 (January 1940): 1.

Swords have always stood for military might. Even some Revolutionary uniform buttons displayed swords. The Boston Independent Company of Militia prescribed buttons "with the motto 'Inimica Tyrannis' and the device of a hand holding a drawn sword, the scabbard thrown and broken." The Sixth Massachusetts Regiment of Continentals wore buttons depicting crossed hunting swords.[2] In families, swords also stirred strong emotional ties to prior generations and their battles. Many appear listed for chosen heirs in eighteenth-century wills.[3] Washington was a collector of swords. He owned at least a dozen.[4]

A buyer of a silver-hilted sword could choose its design. A silversmith might create a unique decorative pattern requested by the customer, or the purchaser could select from a choice of components offered by the maker.[5] There were traditional apolitical designs, but swords fabricated in the colonies in 1775 sometimes displayed decoration that showed the owner's politics. For instance, the silver top mount of the scabbard for the dog-headed sword made in Philadelphia by David Hall disported drums, a cannon, and the flag of the Grand Union, the first national flag

---

2. Don Troiani, *Military Buttons of the American Revolution* (Gettysburg, PA: Thomas Publications, 2001), 121, 125.

3. Neumann, *Swords*, 51; William Stryker documents a silver-hilted sword that was handed down by wills through four generations of his family in first-born son, birthright fashion from 1741 to 1774. William N. Stryker, "Three John Strykers and a Silver-Hilted Sword," *The Genealogical Magazine of New Jersey*, 88 (2013): 50-59.

4. Label on vitrine display of one of Washington's swords, Morristown National Park Museum, Morristown, NJ, July 2012.

5. Neumann, *Swords*, 20; Peterson, *American Sword*, 211.

of 1775-1777.[6] Dog-headed swords, which appeared at the beginning of the war and disappeared soon after it, departed from the long-popular lion-heads and probably embodied anti-British feelings. Political cartoons of the day often depicted dogs harassing Britain. In the accompanying 1778 cartoon detail, with Philadelphia in the background, the British lion lies on the ground asleep, while a dog urinates on him.[7]

The Stout-Moore dog-head sword also displays a motif, and a unique variation of it, whose possible meanings have eluded current

Figure 45. A cartoon detail (1778) of an American dog urinating on the sleeping British lion.

---

6. Hartzler, *Silver Mounted Swords*, 172.

7. "A Picturesque View of the State of the Nation" from *The Westminster Magazine*, February 1778, in Donald H. Cresswell, *The American Revolution in Drawings and Prints* (Washington: The Library of Congress, 1975), 305.

collectors, but whose political message would have been present to many patriots in 1775—to James Moore and Samuel Stout, Jr., and especially to Scots and those who knew John Witherspoon. The guard features in high relief four saltires, an X-shape that, like dog heads, began to appear on some guards around the time of the Revolution and likewise disappeared soon after it.[8] These X's sometimes appear in a decorative row on the edges of guards and usually are viewed simply as a popular geometric pattern of the time. They also ornament the edges of some silver buckles.[9] As mentioned above, in a unique treatment, the Stout-Moore dog-head sword isolates and highlights one of the saltires on the guard in the center of a swirl of spinning rays. [See figure 20]

Among Scottish immigrants and their offspring in the colonies—most of whom were Scotch Irish, sometimes called Ulster-Scots or simply "the Irish"—the saltire, also known as a Saint Andrew's Cross, was a symbol of fierce independence from and armed resistance to the English. The ancient saltire flag of Scotland dates to a Pictish army victory under King Angus McFergus in 832 AD, and a legend that Saint Andrew appeared to Angus in a vision foretelling victory. Andrew, one of the twelve apostles, reportedly was crucified on an X-shaped cross in 69 A.D., not counting himself worthy to be crucified on a cross like that of Jesus. From the ninth century on, the saltire symbolized

---

8. The saltires are seen on silver, especially sword guards, that was produced close to and during the Revolution. The design is found on sword mountings by Ephraim Brasher, John Bailey, William Gilbert, William Moulton, and other unmarked swords of the period. See Hartzler, *Silver Mounted Swords*, 20, 146, 147, 152, 156, 173.

9. Photograph of silver buckle by Thomas Shields, Winterthur Library, Fol. 27; buckle by Shields on display, Philadelphia Museum of Art, June 2015.

Scottish nationalism and independence and flew on flags against the English in many battles. In the time closer to the American Revolution, the saltire flag was raised by the Scottish Presbyterians during the Scottish Revolution of 1638-1644 against the English attempt to force the Church of England on the Scots, and later by the Scottish highlanders in their fight to restore Charles Stuart to the Scottish throne in the Jacobite Rebellion against the English in 1745-46.[10]

A parallel use of the Saint Andrew's Cross was as an alarm during the centuries of warfare in the borderlands between Scotland and England. Scottish highlanders would fasten an X-shaped cross to a pike, set it afire, and ride through the countryside as a call-to-arms. In April 1675, for example, Lauchlan MacLean of Brolas in Mull was accused of gathering four hundred warriors "by sending through the Isle of Mull fyre crosses for convocating of the country people in arms." Such fiery saltires also rallied highlanders as late as the 1745 Jacobite Rebellion.[11]

Only a generation later among the Scotch Irish in America, these customs and memories surrounding the saltire were bound to retain a symbolic grip and transfer to the Revolutionary contest against England. A saltire inscribed on an American sword in 1775 could have conveyed a double meaning, not only a call to armed resistance against the English but also, in the ancient tradition of talisman, a blessing from Saint Andrew. In 1747, the Saint Andrew's Society was founded in Philadelphia to help distressed

---

10. "Saint Andrew and His Flag," http://www.scotshistoryonline.co.uk /saltire/saltire.html. The word "saltire" is Middle French for "stirrup" from the two deltoid shapes that form the cross (like two stirrups).

11. Michael Newton, "The History of the Fiery Cross: Folklore, Literature, and Fakelore," *History Scotland* (May-June 2005): 34-35.

Scottish immigrants, and later its members included no less than five signers of the Declaration of Independence.[12] One was John Witherspoon. His friend Dr. Thomas West Montgomery from Allentown, New Jersey, also became a member.

On his arrival in America from Scotland, Witherspoon joined the Society and afterward preached charity sermons to collect funds for Scottish immigrants.[13] In his 1776 "Address to the Natives of Scotland Residing in America," published with his famous Revolutionary sermon, "The Dominion of Providence over the Affairs of Men," Witherspoon urged the Scots and Scotch Irish to fight for independence.[14]

Between 1763 and 1775, some 55,000 Protestant Irish, later known as the Scotch Irish, arrived in America. They were Presbyterian descendants of Scottish settlers sent to Ireland in the seventeenth century to supplant the local inhabitants of Ulster. Their support of the American Revolution is widely acknowledged. Twenty-five Generals and about a third of the Revolutionary army were Scotch Irish. Their dissenting traditions and frequent location as frontier settlers made them broadly suspicious of central authority.[15]

---

12. "The St. Andrew's Society of Philadelphia: Early Members," http://standrewsociety.org/index2.htm#earlymemb.

13. Varnum Lansing Collins, *President Witherspoon* (New York: Arno Press, 1969, reprint), 148.

14. John Witherspoon, *An Address to the Natives of Scotland Residing in America* (Philadelphia: R. Aitken, 1776).

15. Matthew Dziennik, "Ireland and the American Revolution," *Journal of the American Revolution* (1 May 2014): 5. James Moore's family came to America from Ireland. His ancestors in Kent, England, were accomplices of Thomas Wyatt in the Wyatt insurrection in 1554 in which Protestants rebelled against Catholic Queen Mary's proposed marriage to Catholic King Philip of Spain. In 1554,

A memoir of The Rev. Joseph Campbell (1776-1840), the Ulster-born pastor of Silus Watters at the Pleasant Grove Presbyterian Church near Lebanon, distills their tradition: ". . . for where did Liberty ever gain a field on which the blood of Irishmen did not flow on her behalf? . . . [Ireland's] harp and her sword and her heart's blood have ever been at the service of the oppressed. The soil of Presbyterianism was fatal to the growth of tyranny."[16]

Just across the road from the Pleasant Grove Church, the Jug Tavern did a brisk business. On Independence Day in 1808, "a large crowd [surely including the Watters] gathered there to witness the firing of a large cannon. By some accident, one of the discharges of the gun was premature, and the swab struck Luther Garner, who was standing in front of the piece . . . killing him instantly."[17] Silus Watters may have been carrying the dog-head sword at that abortive celebration.

From the Revolution to the Civil War, Fourth of July celebrations and Washington's Birthday observances were the largest gatherings for festivity and fellowship that most communities witnessed. They included military parades, concerts, sports, bonfires, picnics, illuminations, bells, feasts, orations, and the reading

---

James Moore's ancestor John Moore sold his estate in Kent and with his sons moved to northern Ireland, where the family resided among the Protestant Scotch Irish before emigrating to Massachusetts. James W. Moore, *Rev. John Moore of Newtown*, 6-7.

16. Campbell was the pastor of the Pleasant Grove Presbyterian Church from 1809 to 1832. when the Watters lived in Lebanon Township. Gray, "A Brief Memoir of Joseph Campbell," in *Sermons of the Late Joseph Campbell*, xxiv.

17. Munsell, *History of Morris County*, 378.

of the Declaration of Independence.[18] Heirloom swords and guns were brought down from garrets and over-mantels and carried by parading veterans or their sons.

Music historian James Heintze describes militia bands and fife and drum corps that "provided music for these military, social, and ceremonial events. The bands often led Independence Day parades of military regiments, citizens, and town officials that marched usually in the morning from designated points of assembly, such as taverns, hotels, and court houses, to the churches and other sites where the official ceremonies were held." Such songs as "On Christmas Day in Seventy-Six," which recounted the Battle of Trenton, extolled the heroic efforts of the patriots.[19]

A typical celebration took place near Princeton at Allentown in 1810: "After the ringing of bells and an artillery salute, a procession from Mrs. Forman's house to the Presbyterian Church included a musical ensemble of 'sacred music,' 'an Ode,' and a performance of 'Hail Columbia.' Later, Mrs. Forman provided an 'elegant entertainment' replete with toasts 'amidst discharges of musketry and the resound of martial music.'" [20] In Trenton in 1812, "The celebration of the day was opened with the firing of cannon, the ringing of bells, military music, and the decorations of the dwellings of the citizens on the principal streets.

---

18. Henry S. Laver, "Rethinking the Social Role of the Militia: Community-Building in Antebellum Kentucky," *The Journal of Southern History*, vol. 68, no. 4 (November 2000): 978.

19. James R. Heintze, *Music of the Fourth of July* (Jefferson, NC: McFarland and Company, 2009), 4.

20. "Allentown Celebration," *Trenton Federalist*, July 1810, in Heintze, *Music*, 70.

A procession marched from Warren Street to the Presbyterian Church."[21] These processions with marchers displaying venerable military arms roused memories of days when citizen soldiers defended the nation. They reinvigorated the guiding myths of the Revolution.

As conflicts within the nation presaged civil war, swords once again figured in musical, visual, and literary art as the country reached for heroic Revolutionary ideals to support the Union. The final cohort of Revolutionary veterans were ending their days in the 1850s. Lincoln spoke of "the patriots of seventy-six" as "a forest of giant oaks."[22]

Peter and Ann Watters, my grandfather's grandparents who raised him, loved music. A Kellogg lithograph of "Catherine Hayes, the Swan of Erin" adorned their parlor wall in the 1850s. Born of Protestant parents in Ireland and an international soprano sensation, Hayes (1818-1861) toured America from 1851-1853, sponsored by P.T. Barnum. Peter and Ann may have heard her sing in New Jersey between concerts in New York and Philadelphia.[23]

---

21. *Trenton Federalist*, July 6, 1812, 3, in Heintze, *Music*, 79.

22. "From Lincoln to Washington: A Presidents Day Retrospect," in *America Chapter I* (Colonial Williamsburg Foundation, February 2004), 1; In 1864, The Rev. E. B. Hillard published *The Last Men of the Revolution*, a book of photographs of the supposed last living soldiers of the Revolution. Don Hagist describes the timing and meaning of the book: "The nation, divided by civil war, needed heroes to instill a sense of unity and national pride. . . . No matter how divisive the actual Revolution had been, veterans of that conflict were ideal candidates to be made perfect in the eyes of a public hungry for heroes." Don Hagist, *The Revolution's Last Men: The Soldiers behind the Photographs* (Westholme Publishing, 2015), xviii-xix.

23. See Brian Walsh, *Catherine Hayes: The Hibernian Prima Donna* (Irish Academic Press, 2000). Hayes popularized in America the 1837 ballad "Kathleen

At the same time early in their marriage, they attended week-long winter singing schools and sang from the new tunebook *The Christian Minstrel* by J. B. Aiken of Philadelphia.[24]

Peter and Ann surely heard the 1855 popular ballad "The Sword of Bunker Hill," written by William Ross Wallace (1819-1881), son of a Scottish Presbyterian minister, and whose intensely patriotic poetry was praised by Edgar Allen Poe. The text of the song presents a dying Revolutionary veteran whose last request is to hold again "the sword of Bunker Hill":

'Oh, Keep the sword,'—his accents broke—
A smile—and he was dead!
His wrinkled hand still grasped the blade
Upon that dying bed.
The son remains; the sword remains—
Its glory growing still—
And twenty millions bless the sire,
And sword of Bunker Hill.

The ballad was a favorite among Civil War Union troops. Wallace's poetry showed a mythical reverence for the Revolution, calling it an "era sublime" and Washington a "savior" of his country.[25]

Mavourneen."

24. J. B. Aiken, *The Christian Minstrel, Designed for the Use of Churches, Singing Schools, and Societies* (Philadelphia: T. K. Collins, 1854), author's collection.

25. "William Wallace," http://xroads.virginia.edu/~class/am485_97/revolution/William.html; "The Sword of Bunker Hill," music composed by Bernard Covert, words by William Ross Wallace (Cleveland: S. Brainard's Sons, 1855), author's collection.

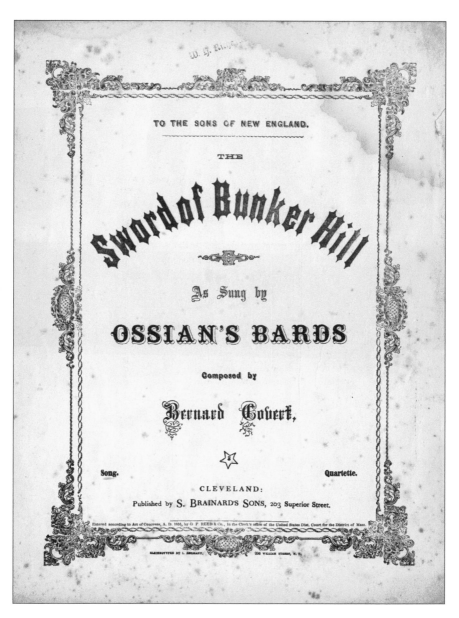

Figure 46. The cover of sheet music, "The Sword of Bunker Hill," 1855. Ossian was a legendary Irish poet whose work purportedly appeared in Scottish Gaelic ballads.

Henry Wadsworth Longfellow (1807-1882) joined composer Wallace in revivifying Revolutionary narratives during the Civil War. Twice in *Tales of a Wayside Inn*, in the "Prelude" and in the "Interlude" bracketing "The Landlord's Tale: Paul Revere's Ride," Longfellow highlights the patriot sword hanging on the parlor wall, "dim with dust" yet "glimmering with a latent light." Written in 1860, "Paul Revere's Ride" appeared in Longfellow's *Tales of a Wayside Inn* in 1863, a project he undertook to combat his personal struggles during the war and his grief over his son's injuries while serving in the Army of the Potomac.[26] David Hackett Fischer asserts, "The insistent beat of Longfellow's meter reverberated through the North like a drum roll. . . . This was a call to arms for a new American generation in another moment of peril."[27]

The memories and meanings of the dog-head sword slipped and changed into the 1860s, until Peter and Ann Watters took it with them from Lebanon to Succasunna in 1869. They began to raise my grandfather Lawrence Watters in the 1870s. My grandfather's memory preserved a thread of the sword story, but the whole cloth had vanished by his day.

A decade after publication of *Tales of a Wayside Inn*, during the Centennial celebrations of 1876, the Watters toured the Ford Mansion, Washington's Headquarters, in Morristown. The house recently had been purchased and opened by the Washington Association. Peter and Ann Watters bought one of the first souvenirs

---

26. Robert L. Gale, *A Henry Wadsworth Longfellow Companion* (Westport, CT: Greenwood Press, 2003), 258-259.

27. David Hackett Fischer, *Paul Revere's Ride* (New York: Oxford University Press, 1994), 331.

Figure 47. The frontispiece of the first edition (1863) of Longfellow's *Tales of a Wayside Inn*, with a sword over the fireplace mantel "glimmering with a latent light."

Figure 48. The page turner made from an original roof
shingle of the Ford Mansion, Morristown, with transfer print
of the Mansion. Sold by the Washington Association of New
Jersey and purchased by the Watters in the 1870s.

the Association sold, a wooden page-turner allegedly made from
an Atlantic white cedar shingle that had roofed the house when
Washington slept there.[28] It was wood that sheltered Washington
from the snow and ice of the bitter winter of 1779-1780. It was
wood that witnessed the visit of the Marquis de Lafayette in May
1780, when he brought news that the French were sending more
ships to aid the American cause. It was a "relick" that, like the
sword, enabled the Watters "to commune with men and things
of other times."[29]

---

28. Collection of the author. The page-turner is Mauchline Ware (or a copy
of it), made in the area of Mauchline, East Ayrshire, Scotland, from the 1850s
to 1933. Popular among Victorians, small decorative and utilitarian items were
made of sycamore wood adorned with transfer-ware scenes and covered with multiple layers of copal varnish. Some objects were made of wood from specific historic structures. In this case, the wood purportedly came from the original Ford
Mansion shingles.

29. Keim, "Remembering the 'Olden Time,'" in Boudreau and Lovell, *A
Material World*, 294.

Epilogue

O n June 17, 1825, the fiftieth anniversary of the Battle of Bunker Hill, the Marquis de Lafayette laid the cornerstone of the Bunker Hill Monument in Charlestown, Massachusetts. Stories of the battle told by elderly veterans present were recorded in notebooks. In 1842, historian George Ellis read the narratives. He described many of the accounts as "mixtures of old men's broken memories, fond imaginings, and love of the marvelous."[30]

My search for the sword encountered all of these foibles, but looking at the surviving documents from a greater distance, what we can say with considerable certainty is that no appropriate owner of the sword with the initials JM other than James Moore appears in the life of Silus Watters. The sword is an officer's sword. Such swords were expensive and uncommon. A web of family and social relationships connected Captain James Moore and Silus Watters. The patrons of Silus Watters' tavern augmented those associations. In the years immediately after the Revolution, primarily objects that belonged to its famous leaders were prized.[31] James Moore was a hero in the Princeton community. Silus

---

30. *Massachusetts Historical Society Proceedings*, 2 (1880), 231.

31. Teresa Barrett, *Sacred Relics: Pieces of the Past in Nineteenth-Century America* (Chicago: University of Chicago Press, 2013), 79-80.

Watters knew both the hero, who was his own captain, and the probable maker of the sword, Samuel Stout, Jr., his neighbor and fellow soldier. As a tavern keeper, Silus Watters also was an important person respected by his peers, a worthy recipient of the sword. James Moore and Silus Watters were lifelong friends, and Moore died childless. Silus moved away from Princeton in 1791/1792, the year that Phebe Moore, wife of James' youth, died. James may have given his sword to Silus at that time as a parting gift, a token of shared memories and gratitude for Silus's friendship. When the sword was removed from its community of origin, its commonly known connection to its wartime hero was left behind and eventually forgotten by the descendants of his friend.

The history of James Moore and Silus Watters that we know allows us, like the veterans of Bunker Hill, to indulge our imagination, perhaps with firmer historical footing, and remember whom and what the dog saw:

A young journeyman punching and burnishing silver into sight; Princeton militia marching to their captain's chant; James Moore's stinking tannery; John Witherspoon preaching— Richard and Annis Stockton, Elias Boudinot, Benjamin Rush, Philip Fithian, Samuel Stout, Jr., Silus Watters listening; the Declaration of Independence read aloud in front of Nassau Hall illuminated by tallow dips in all the windows, dubious slaves among the excited crowd.

General George Washington and Thomas Paine riding into and retreating through Newark; dark waters of the Delaware River in December 1776; a captured turkey dinner; Alexander Hamilton firing a cannon; the broken front door of Nassau Hall; surrendered regulars skulking; freed Princeton prisoners exulting.

Militia wading the Millstone River under enemy cannon fire at the Battle of Millstone; unnamed sharp skirmishes in the Forage Wars; restive prisoners and languishing sick and wounded in Nassau Hall; smoke and fog and rifle fire at the Chew Mansion at the Battle of Germantown; Governor William Livingston under protective guard in 1777; British prisoners from the Battle of Monmouth trudging to Philadelphia; General Baron Von Steuben drilling troops at Springfield; General Anthony Wayne negotiating with Pennsylvania Line mutineers.

Toasts and cannon salutes at Beekman's Tavern, Professor William Houston orating, Princeton village illuminated—all celebrating victory at Yorktown in 1781; Governor Livingston and his wife, Susannah French Livingston, hosts at an April 1783 ball in Trenton marking peace with Britain; Commander-in-Chief George Washington and members of Congress on stage at the September 1783 college commencement in the Presbyterian Church; bright light of Independence Day processions; dim light and dust of a century in Lebanon and Succasunna garrets; a grandfather showing his grandson: "This sword was used in the Revolutionary War."

Index

All place names are in New Jersey, unless otherwise indicated.

Note on the Author

John Lawrence Brasher, PhD, a native of New Jersey, is Denson N. Franklin Professor of Religion Emeritus at Birmingham-Southern College. Educated at Duke University and Yale University, he has written books on American religion, music, and traditional material culture. His interests and publications also include environmental ethics, botany, folklore, archeology, and historic preservation. He can be contacted by email at lbrasher@bsc.edu.

CPSIA information can be obtained
at www.ICGtesting.com
Printed in the USA
BVHW022017280221
601270BV00006B/14